First World War
and Army of Occupation
War Diary
France, Belgium and Germany

48 DIVISION
Divisional Troops
Divisional Ammunition Column
1 April 1915 - 31 October 1917

WO95/2750/4

The Naval & Military Press Ltd
www.nmarchive.com
Published in association with The National Archives

Published by

The Naval & Military Press Ltd

Unit 10 Ridgewood Industrial Park,

Uckfield, East Sussex,

TN22 5QE England

Tel: +44 (0) 1825 749494

www.naval-military-press.com

www.nmarchive.com

This diary has been reprinted in facsimile from the original. Any imperfections are inevitably reproduced and the quality may fall short of modern type and cartographic standards.

© **Crown Copyright**
Images reproduced by permission of The National Archives, London, England, 2015.

Contents

Document type	Place/Title	Date From	Date To
Heading	WO95/2750/4		
Heading	48th Division 48th Divl Ammn Col. Apr 1915-Oct 1917		
Heading	Divl Ammn "Col" 48th (SM) Division Vol I 1-30.4.15		
Heading	War Diary Of Sth Mid Divl Amm. Col. From 1st April 15 To 30 April 15 Volume IX		
War Diary		01/04/1915	30/04/1915
Heading	War Diary of 48th (Sth Mid) Divl Amm Col From 1st May 1915-31st May 1915 Volume II		
War Diary		01/05/1915	31/05/1915
Heading	War Diary Of Divisional Ammunition Column 48th Division From1 June 1915 To 30 June 1915 Volume III		
War Diary		01/06/1915	30/06/1915
Heading	War Diary Of 48th (Sth Mid) Divisional Ammunition Column From 1st July 1915-31st July 1915 Volume IV		
War Diary		01/07/1915	31/07/1915
Heading	48th Division 48th Divl Amm Col Aug 15 Vol V		
Heading	War Diary Of 48th (South Mid) Divl Ammn Col From 1st August 1915-31st August 1915 Volume XIII		
War Diary		01/08/1915	31/08/1915
Heading	48th Division 48th Divl Ammn Col Sept 1915 Vol VI		
Heading	War Diary Of 48th (South Mid) Divisional Ammn Colmn From 1st Sept 1915-30th Sept 1915 Volume XIV		
War Diary		01/09/1915	30/09/1915
Heading	48th Division 48th Divl Ammn Col. Oct 15 Vol VII		
Heading	War Diary Of 48th (South Mid) Divisional Ammunition Column From 1st October 1915 To 31st October 1915 Volume XV		
War Diary		01/10/1915	31/10/1915
Heading	War Diary Of 48th (S.M.) Divl Ammn Column From 1st November 1915-30th Nov 1915 Volume VIII		
War Diary	In The Field	01/11/1915	30/11/1915
Heading	48th Divl Ammn Col. Dec Vol IX		
War Diary	In The Field	01/12/1915	31/12/1915
Heading	War Diary Of 48th Divisional Ammunition Column From 1st January To 31st January 1916 Volume X		
War Diary	In The Field	01/01/1916	31/01/1916
Heading	War Diary Of 48th Divisional Ammunition Column From 1st To 29th February 1916 Volume XI		
War Diary	In The Field	01/02/1916	29/02/1916
Heading	War Diary Of 48th (South Midland) Divisional Ammunition Column R.F.A. From 1st March 1916 To 31st March 1916 Volume XII		
War Diary	In The Field	01/03/1916	31/03/1916
Miscellaneous	Divisional Ammunition Column		
War Diary	In The Field	01/04/1916	30/04/1916
Heading	War Diary 48th (South Midland) Divisional Ammunition Column R.F.A. May 1916 Volume 14		
War Diary	In The Field	01/05/1916	31/05/1916

Heading	War Diary 48th (South Midland) Divisional Ammunition Column June 1916 Volume XIX		
War Diary	In The Field	01/06/1916	30/06/1916
Heading	War Diary July 1916 48th S.M. Divisional Ammunition Column R.F.A. Volume 16		
War Diary	In The Field	01/07/1916	31/07/1916
Heading	48th (South Midland) Divisional Artillery 48th Divisional Ammunition Column R.F.A. August 1916		
War Diary	In The Field	01/08/1916	31/08/1916
Heading	48th Division 48th Divisional Ammunition Column September 1916		
War Diary		01/09/1916	30/09/1916
Heading	War Diary Of 48th (South Mid) Divisional Ammuntion Column R.F.A. For November 1916 Volume20		
War Diary	In The Field	01/11/1916	30/11/1916
Heading	War Diary Of 48th (South Midland) Divisional Ammunition Column R.F.A. Month of December 1916 Volume 21		
War Diary	In The Field	01/12/1916	31/12/1916
Heading	War Diary Of 48th (S.M.) Divisional Ammunition Column R.F.A. For January 1917 Volume XXV		
War Diary	In The Field	01/01/1917	31/01/1917
Heading	War Diary Of 48th (South Midland) Divisional Ammunition Column R.F.A. For The Month Of February 1917 Volume XXVII		
War Diary	In The Field	01/02/1917	28/02/1917
Heading	War Diary March 1917 48 Divisional Ammunition Column		
War Diary	In The Field	01/03/1917	31/03/1917
Heading	War Diary Of 48th (S.M) Divisional Ammunition Column R.F.A. For Month Of April 1917 Volume XXIX		
War Diary	Courcelles	01/04/1917	01/04/1917
War Diary	Tincourt	02/04/1917	17/04/1917
War Diary	Villers Faucon	18/04/1917	30/04/1917
Heading	War Diary Of 48th (S.M.) Divisional Ammunition Column R.F.A. For May 1917 Volume XXX		
War Diary	Villers Faucon	01/05/1917	01/05/1917
War Diary	Buire	02/05/1917	15/05/1917
War Diary	Le Transloy	16/05/1917	19/05/1917
War Diary	Haplincourt	20/05/1917	21/05/1917
War Diary	Beugny	22/05/1917	31/05/1917
Heading	War Diary Of 48th (S.M.) Divisional Ammunition Column R.F.A. From 1st June 1917 To 30th June 1917 (Volume XXXI)		
War Diary	Beugny	01/06/1917	23/06/1917
War Diary	Bottom Wood Near Mametz	24/06/1917	30/06/1917
Heading	War Diary For 48th (S.M.) Divisional Ammunition Column RFA For The Month of July 1917 Volume XXXII		
War Diary	Bottom Wood Nr Mametz	01/07/1917	04/07/1917
War Diary	Beaussart	05/07/1917	05/07/1917
War Diary	Thievres	06/07/1917	06/07/1917
War Diary	Cannettemont	07/07/1917	07/07/1917
War Diary	Roellecourt	08/07/1917	09/07/1917
War Diary	Nedon Nedonchelle	10/07/1917	10/07/1917

War Diary	Boeseghem	11/07/1917	11/07/1917
War Diary	Staple	12/07/1917	12/07/1917
War Diary	Steenvoorde	13/07/1917	13/07/1917
War Diary	Peselhoek	14/07/1917	31/07/1917
Heading	War Diary August 1917 48th (S.M) Divisional Ammunition Column R.F.A. Volume XXXIV		
War Diary	Vlamertinghe	01/08/1917	31/08/1917
Heading	War Diary For Month Of September 1917 48 Divl Ammn Column R.F.A. Volume No. XXXV		
War Diary	Vlamertinghe	01/09/1917	28/09/1917
War Diary	Noordpene	29/09/1917	30/09/1917
Heading	War Diary Of 48th (SM) Divisional Ammunition Column R.F.A. For October 1917 Volume XXXV		
War Diary	Noordpene	01/10/1917	03/10/1917
War Diary	Winnezeele	04/10/1917	05/10/1917
War Diary	Brandhoek	06/10/1917	08/10/1917
War Diary	Vlamertinghe	09/10/1917	13/10/1917
War Diary	Eecke	14/10/1917	14/10/1917
War Diary	Morbecque	15/10/1917	15/10/1917
War Diary	Vendin-Lez-Bethune	16/10/1917	17/10/1917
War Diary	Ablain-St-Nazaire	18/10/1917	22/10/1917
War Diary	La Targette	23/10/1917	26/10/1917
War Diary	Mont St Eloi	27/10/1917	31/10/1917

Washington
Worksheet 4

48TH DIVISION

BEF

48TH DIVL AMMN COL. OCT 1917
APR 1915-~~MAR 1919~~

TO ITALY

121/5254

Dis l'Armie "Col. 48th (SM) Division

Vol I — 30.4.15
Nov '19

Confidential.
War Diary.
of.
Sth Mid. Divl. Amm. Col.
from 1st April. 15 to 30th April '15
Volume IX.

Army Form C. 2118.

WAR DIARY
or
INTELLIGENCE SUMMARY.   5th Cnd Divl Ammn Col.
(Erase heading not required.)

Instructions regarding War Diaries and Intelligence Summaries are contained in F. S. Regs., Part II. and the Staff Manual respectively. Title pages will be prepared in manuscript.

Place	Date	Hour	Summary of Events and Information	Remarks and references to Appendices
	1/14/15		Hd Qrs Cdn DAC arrived at Havre on "Anglo Canadian" at 12 noon. - Hd Qrs & 1st See left Havre Point 6 at 9.9 p.m. -	
	2d "		Arrived CASSEL 4 pm. - met by Gen Butler. Other Sections arrived during night.	
	3 "		Staff Captain came over & (visited) Column at 9 a.m. to billeting area near HAZEBROUCK.	
	4 "		Requiring Entrances to fields etc. C.O. to Hd Qrs at CAESTRE & new billet.	
	5 "		Received orders to move to new area near MERRIS.	
	6 "		Moved in direction of MERRIS – were then ordered by Staff Captain to proceed to NOOTE BOOM	
	7 "		C.O. & Adj to MERRIS & see A.D.V.S. & D.Q.O.	
	8 "		Inspection of all horses by C.O.	
	9 "		Gen Butler came over	
	10 "		Staff Capt came over & took Adj. for new billets near MERRIS.	
	11 "		Looking for billets to move to.	
	12 "		Received orders to move at once to furnish 1 mile south of MERRIS. Gen Butler & Brig Maj. came over in morning. C.O., Adj., & Capts BURBIDGE, PRITCHETT, WOTTON attended Gesture by Brig Maj. on Court Martials at Hd Qrs RA. 36 remounts received.	
	13 "		D.C. DA Park came over re 15 pdr Amn. – Remounts issued to various brigades	
	14 "			
	15 "		R4 Hd Qrs moved to NIEPPE.	
	16 "		Returns, letters, etc drawn from LA CRECHE for 1st time –	
	17 "		——	
	18 "		Ammn inspection Amn 2, 3 Sections & deficiencies made up.	
	19 "		do — do — 1–4 do.	
	20 "		—— do — Ady to Metro Work for new billeting area which was not approved	
	21 "		Staff Capt, O.C., Adj. to Metro Work for new billeting area which was not approved Capt PRITCHETT, Lest HOPKINS, CROSS & SELBY-LOWNDES attached temporarily to various brigades	

WAR DIARY
or
INTELLIGENCE SUMMARY.

Army Form C. 2118.

Place	Date	Hour	Summary of Events and Information	Remarks and references to Appendices
	22/4/16		Adj. to NIEPPE to draw cash.	
	23 "		Marching drill etc.	
	24 "		Full marching order parade - harness fitting.	
	25 "		Gen. Butler came & inspected camp.	
	28 "		Officers note, & funeral venture - Capt HANKINS O.C. DA Park came over	
	29 "		Notice received that L. CROSS in the attached to Park.	
	30 "		C.O. & Adj. to NIEPPE to R.A. Hd Qrs	

Wyndham
CAPT., ADJT.
1/1ST STH. MID. DIVL. AMMUNITION COLUMN.

48th Division

Confidential

121/5775

War Diary
of
48th (Sth Mid) Divl Ammn Col.
from 1st May - 1915 — 31st May 1915

Volume X II

48th Division

Army Form C. 2118.

WAR DIARY
INTELLIGENCE SUMMARY.
(Erase heading not required.)

Place	Date	Hour	Summary of Events and Information	Remarks and references to Appendices
	1 Aug 15		O.C., Adjt. to BAILLEUL to arrange with 3rd Corps Spec. Off. to find & secure billets for the Unit.	
	3 "		Billet marking party made. O.C. Adjt. to NIEPPE & Hd Qr RA.	
	4 "		Lt HOPKINS returns from attachment to 1st Hd FA Bde - Hd Qr. & the 6 Sec. to NIEPPE to cut fodder.	
	5 "		Capt BURBIDGE went for attachment to 1st SM FA Bde.	
	6 "		Capt PRITCHETT returns from attachment to 3rd SM FA Bde. Lt WICKS went for attachment to 3rd SM FA Bde.	
	7 "		8 mules received - 1 F.S. wagon horses & harness for carrying parades -	
	10 "		C.O. - Adjt to Hd Qr RA. Col Harris ADVS. inspects all horses - Capt WOTTON went to 2nd SM FA Bde for attachment. Lt SELBY LOWNDES returns from attachment to 4th SM FA (How) Bde - Bvy Fmr Ross-JOHNSON appointed C.R.A.	
	11 "		Capt BURBIDGE returns from attachment to 1st SM FA Bde.	
	12 "		C.O. - Adjt to NIEPPE meet new C.R.A.	
	13 "		Gen KEIR came to tea	
	14 "		Inspection of all horses by C.O. Lt WICKS returns from attachment to 3rd SM FA Bde.	
	15 "		C.O. - Adjt to travel with Gen KEIR - & Hd Qr RA in afternoon - Remainder of 5" How Ammunition Park over to 4th DA Park.	

Wheyham
CAPT. ADJT.
48th (STH. MID.) DIVL. AMMUNITION COLUMN.

Army Form C. 2118.

WAR DIARY
or
INTELLIGENCE SUMMARY.
(Erase heading not required.)

Instructions regarding War Diaries and Intelligence Summaries are contained in F. S. Regs., Part II. and the Staff Manual respectively. Title pages will be prepared in manuscript.

Place	Date	Hour	Summary of Events and Information	Remarks and references to Appendices
	19 May 15		Lt. SELBY-LOWNDES attended Medical Board at NIEPPE with reference to commission in Regular Army.	
	21"		O.C. & Adjt. to return group at 6 am. Received orders in evening to proceed to new area nr. FLETRE.	
	22"		Moved to new area 2 mile S. of FLETRE by 12 pm. Staff Captain came over.	
	24		Gas effects felt for 1st Time. Respirators tested for.	
	25		Col. HARRIS ADVS inspected all horses. Hd Qrs wired that Lt. SELBY-LOWNDES to go to 3rd Cav. Fd. Rde. Trsp. for casualty.	
	26		Adjt to NIEPPE. Informed by Staff Captain that DAC would move to new area BAILLEUL – NIEPPE road. Supply Ammn. & Brigade Columns Received orders to attach.	
	27		Transfer of Ammunition from Park completed by 7 am. Wired Hd Qr R.A. accordingly.	
	28		C.O. & Staff Captain to see proprietors billets in new area.	
	29		C.O. & Adjt to see new billets. Received orders to move tomorrow.	
	30		Moved to new area on BAILLEUL – NIEPPE road, all return in by 1.30 pm.	

Wyndham
CAPT. ADJT.
5TH MID DIVL. AMMUNITION COLUMN

WAR DIARY
or
INTELLIGENCE SUMMARY.

Army Form C. 2118.

Place	Date	Hour	Summary of Events and Information	Remarks and references to Appendices
	30th	am/pm	1st CROSS reported from 46th D.A.C - attached to 2nd Res. 25 tents drawn from 3rd Cpt Ordnance STEENWERCK. Drew ammunition from divisional section of Park	
	31st		Inspection of vehicles by C.O. Col HARRIS from 1st DARLING & horses afterwards of 2nd F.Amb at BAILLEUL	

W. Wykeham
CAPT., ADJT.
1/1st (STH. MID.) DIVL. AMMUNITION COLUMN.

48th Division

CONFIDENTIAL
181/6015

WAR DIARY

of

Divisional Ammunition Column.
48th Division.

from 1 June 1915 to 30 June 1915

VOLUME ~~II~~ III

Army Form C. 2118.

WAR DIARY
or
INTELLIGENCE SUMMARY.
(Erase heading not required.)

Instructions regarding War Diaries and Intelligence Summaries are contained in F.S. Regs., Part II. and the Staff Manual respectively. Title pages will be prepared in manuscript.

Place	Date	Hour	Summary of Events and Information	Remarks and references to Appendices
	1 Nov. 1915.		Sections inspected by C.O. A.D.O.S. and D.A.A. & Q.M.G. visited D.A.C. in afternoon.	
	2		Lectures inspected by C.O. C.O. & Adjt. visited R.A. Hd. Qrs at NIEPPE	
	3		Som horses strayed from No. 3 section. Reported same to R.A. HdQrs. 5 horses sent to stable of Nt Section	
	4		Adjutant of NIEPPE to D.A.A.S. Cash. Nos. 1 & 2 sections visited by Co. & firing horse died in No. 2 section	
	5		Brig. Gen. Ron Johnson inspected 3 & 4 sections with Brig. Major. Officers musketry practise in afternoon	
	6		Sections visited by Co. in morning. Non Conformist church parade held at 4 p.m.	
	7		C.O. & Adjt. to NIEPPE to see D.A.D.O.S. Brig. Gen. Van Shaw brigade this side held at Hd Qrs all day.	
	8		Alarm at 10 pm for Nos 1 & 2 sections to practise Practise alarm for No. 3 & 4 sections 3. A.M. After Exercise P.M.O. on inspected Camp. Baggage wagon.	
	9		horses inspected by C.O. & Adjutant. Two wagons loaded over to A.S.C. Establishment of S.A.A. reduced to 720 ans pr. round. 1 wagon	
	10		Went to 114 Bde. No. 2 section word to raise pids. Loan for N.C.O's given No. 4 section stopped for neglect of stable duties	
	11		by Brig. Gen. Fanshawe & Brig. Gen. Ron Johnson inspected whole of D.A.C. Brig. Ja. Fanshawe afterwards addressed its men	
	12		C.O. & Adjt. to NIEPPE. Rec'd orders to relieve all untrained gunners by Park.	
	13		Harness inspection. No. 2 section. 11 A.M. Church parade at 3 p.m. under Chaplain McNeill	
	14		C.O. & Adjt. to NIEPPE with Devil Field Am. Park. Reported shortage of sealed pairs.	
	16		Lt. Cross sent to No. 1 section. Lt. Hopkins to No. 2 section.	

WAR DIARY
or
INTELLIGENCE SUMMARY.
(Erase heading not required.)

Army Form C. 2118.

Instructions regarding War Diaries and Intelligence Summaries are contained in F. S. Regs., Part II. and the Staff Manual respectively. Title pages will be prepared in manuscript.

Place	Date	Hour	Summary of Events and Information	Remarks and references to Appendices
	17 Nov		Lieut Carl Smith Port NIEPPE for repairs relieved her attached to Co. Adjt attended F.E.C.M. at Hd Qn. 2 S.M.F.A. Bde Lieut WICKS a member of the Court.	
	18.		Capt HEWITT reported for duty with No 3 Section. No 4 Section inspected at 4 P.M. No 2 section inspected at 5.30 P.M. Shoeing in this section found to be very bad.	
	19.		Farrier Sergt. Ren. Inns to No. 2 Section to supervise shoeing. Capt T.B. PRITCHETT to 3" S.M.F.A. Bde.	
	20.		Lee marched to Halts at Port NIEPPE	
	21.		Q.L.D. Petershaws Draws. He reported to have sarcoptic mange.	
	22.		Nos 3 & 4 Sections took march State.	
	23.		Capts CROWSHAY & CHANDLER on 12 Bombs, number of Issues 4 hours for No 8 section & 6 No 4 section.	
	24.		Received orders for mar.	
	25.		Capt A. WYREKAM reported Bnl Hd Qrs as temporary A.O.C. to Major FANSHAWE	
	26.		J.A.C. Sligho Capt. Inspected 5 Lieut Sen PULTENEY in BAILLEUL & MAG Run FANSHAWE	
	27.		just outside VIEUX BERQUIN	
	28.		Co. reparted to 144th Bde HdQrs Orders to march at 6 p.m. Column marched to North of ROBECQ na MERVILLE & CALONNE arriving 11.30 p.m.	
	29.		Column worn off at 6 p.m. Inspected by Brig. Gen. McPHERSON who said he was well pleased with the appearance of the Column. arrived at FERFAY 11.30 P.M.	
	30.		Horses noted watering arrangements used. Issue 30 rounds 5" Harshell & 33,000 S.A.A. from park.	

L.D. Meere Capt.
O.C. 48th Dist. Ams. Co

48th Division

Confidential

121/6243

WAR DIARY
OF
48th (Sth Mid) DIVISIONAL AMMUNITION COLUMN.

from 1st July: 1915 — 31st July 1915.

Volume XII. IV

WAR DIARY
or
INTELLIGENCE SUMMARY.
(Erase heading not required.)

Army Form C. 2118.

Instructions regarding War Diaries and Intelligence Summaries are contained in F. S. Regs., Part II. and the Staff Manual respectively. Title pages will be prepared in manuscript.

Place	Date	Hour	Summary of Events and Information	Remarks and references to Appendices
	1 July		Inspection by O.C. Visit from Staff Major R.A.	
	2 July		Visit from G.O.C.R.A. who expressed satisfaction. Horse exercise in afternoon. Horses exchanged with 5th Bar. Battery.	
	3 July		O.C. President of Enq. Married at Hq. of S.M.F.A.I.S.	
	4 July		Horse exercise. Capt. Stanley A.S.C. inspected baggage wagon horses - satisfied. New watering place selected owing to failure of original one owing to supply. Voluntary Church parade at 6.45 p.m.	
	5 July		Ten Falconers and Staff inspected Camps at 8.30 am. C. Dan Co. & 88 S.C.R.H. at Liters. F.O.C.H.Y & U.H.Y. IT taps. Return 1 wagon needed for 12,000 tombs. Return dept in Keenig. 12 Calpas, 2 Sgts, 27 men formed O.M.S. from Dir Park - Sgt Mother 3rd Dec to O.M.S. Inner Sgts. Sgt Cockrum 1st Section - 2nd section. Enfinden Seare	
	6 July		Later Ouffly paired. OC arranged different places for each section.	(Column inspected)
	7 July		P.o.Y. officer visited column re been forage.	
	8 July		Horse exercise and inspection by Co.	
	9 July		All section inspected by Co.	
	10 July		O.C. visited Amm. Park & ce amm. Supply.	

WAR DIARY
or
INTELLIGENCE SUMMARY.

Army Form C. 2118.

Place	Date	Hour	Summary of Events and Information	Remarks and references to Appendices
	11 July		500 rounds New 15p'r Amm'n rec'd from Park.	
	12 July		Church Parade 9 + 5 A.M. at Chateau under Senior Chaplain S Walters drew bombs. Received intimation of move. In readiness all day orders subsequently received for Photing day.	
	13 July		O.C. on leave to England. Capt. Andrew Lewis in Command.	
	15 July		Court Martial on Dvr Hancox and Rogers	
	17 July		— Sentence promulgated.	
	18 July		Order to move received.	
	20 July		Column moved off Notton 7am Berquist Station 9 am 15p-14 each sec 1 left Oxton at 4. 10.p.m. arrived Doullens 9. 3.p.m. Detrained & marched to Authie. (AUTHIE)	
	21 July		Arrived AUTHIE 3.30. A.M. Marched Stamp E of AUTHIE at 2 p.m. Remainder arrived AUTHIE as follows No 1 5.30 A.M. No.2 8 A.M. No 3 12 p.m. No 4 6.30 p.m.	
	22 July		All horse inspected by Co. & V.O. All 15p'r Amm'n returned to Amm Park	
	23 July		Filled up with 4 536 rds. of 18 p dr. BSM Earl & Sgt I Siffer obtained from team.	

Army Form C. 2118.

WAR DIARY
or
INTELLIGENCE SUMMARY.
(Erase heading not required.)

Instructions regarding War Diaries and Intelligence Summaries are contained in F.S. Regs., Part II and the Staff Manual respectively. Title pages will be prepared in manuscript.

Hour, Date, Place	Summary of Events and Information	Remarks and references to Appendices
July 24	Rec'd 6 G.S. Wagons from Amm Col: 1st S.M.F.A.S.Ae	
July 25	15 pr. Gun Stores returned. Evidence for Court Martial on A/L. ELTON taken. Celebration of Holy Communion at 9.30am by Gallan McNulty.	
July 26	Capt. E. IC SAUNDERS reported to Adjutant. O.C. to HEBUTERNE & Bois A & B to Divn Ammn	
July 27	O.C. saw C.R.A. re new dispol. of C. and adj. to SARTON by 10 pm for Column forming, 2 ration cart to 1/2 SMB.5ke for Divn for resting.	
July 28	Court Martial on A/L ELTON.	
July 29	- Promulgated by Adjutant. 20 men & 2 NCOs	
July 30	16 Panthers in permanent Hard fastine. France Aug 1 to 2nd SMFA FA Ale to Timber a/c. Same inspected by O.C.	
July 31	H.Q. lines moved to Adjacent field. AUTHIE or ... finished by O.C. & Sect. Commander for Winter Camps.	

[signature] Capt. & Adjutant
Aug 1/15

D/7435

48th Division

48th Div. Ammn. Col.

Aug. 15

Vol I

Confidential

WAR DIARY
OF
48th (South Mid) Divl Ammn Col:

From 1st August 1915 — 31st August 1915.

Volume XIII

Army Form C. 2118.

WAR DIARY
or
INTELLIGENCE SUMMARY.
(Erase heading not required.)

Instructions regarding War Diaries and Intelligence Summaries are contained in F. S. Regs., Part II. and the Staff Manual respectively. Title pages will be prepared in manuscript.

Place	Date Aug	Hour	Summary of Events and Information	Remarks and references to Appendices
	1.		18 Men proceeded on Aug leave. 12 h. Bus. 6 h. Steeged. Voluntary Church Parade. 3 p.m. Chaplain McNaile.	
	2.		6 Men assisting local farmers. Staff Captain & 20 Maintenance Jonica	
	3.		O.C. Bde SAOMC M. Coal fatigue & bulletin. SOCRA RE Major & Chaplain to dinner.	
	4.		O.C. + Adjt. 6 Bde Columns re SAA	
	5.		O.C. + Adjt. to 4 S.M.Bde in action	
	8.		40 men to 3 S.M.Bde for 18.88 ag. O.T. to CB & RA re O.C. No 2 Section	
	9.		40 men 3.S.M.Bde. O.C. + OC No2 Section to see QCRA. 230	
	10.		Hon. A No 4 Section Cooks LCs women to 3 S.M.Bde.	
	11.		48 Men on leave. 70 Men to Doullens to Remount park. Major Ross Griffith interviews Candidates for Tunneling Corps.	
	12.		40 men 6.3. S.M.Bde.	
	13.		60 men 6.5.S.M.Bde. O.C. & NO An. 2.3. 4 Men re interchange of officers	
	14.		60 men to 3 S.M.Bde. FGCM. 8 Pritchard. Horse died 6 No 3 Section.	
	15.		LT Ross took a Lieut. Church parade. 4.30. Capt. Richey MS. Capt. Perkins Forsman attached	
	16.		Adjt returned from leave. O.C. took Offrs re Screening	
	17.		O.C. BSM Bourne to 4 S.M.Bde in action.	
	18.		O.C. & Adjt. 6 4 S.M.Bde in column	
	19.		Lieut Hunter left at 10 AM. Sergt Blake % Coal fatigue	
	20.		O.C. Inspected No 3 Section. Showing my brad. SAA. MK B. returns from infantry & exchanged.	
	21.		SAA Still being returned and exchanged. Church parade. 4. Box for officers dinner 5.30. under W.H.Moon	
	22.		All over in billets	
	24.		SAOMC on M. bulletin a bulletin – Authie	
	25.		O.C. to 4 SM Bde.	
	26.		Bulletin for A. Q. No 1 & 3. Bde undertaken LDAC	
	28.		Capt Murchyn & Lieut Gatticcar reported from 5 th Kallers	
	29.		No 3 Harness soon fitted up	
	30.		To The FGRSB M. Gatting B. A. Co. Ptan	

LT-COL

COMMAND: 4.8" DIV. AMMUNITION COLUMN.

1577 Wt. W10791/1773 50,000 1/15 D.D. & L. A.D.S.S./Forms/C. 2118.

31/7435

48th Virain

48th Div. Ammn. Col.

Sep 1915

Vol VI

Confidential

WAR DIARY
OF
48th (South Mid) Divisional Amm:n Col:mn

From 1st Sept: 1915 — 30th Sept: 1915.

VOLUME XIV

WAR DIARY
or
INTELLIGENCE SUMMARY.
(Erase heading not required.)

Army Form C. 2118.

Instructions regarding War Diaries and Intelligence Summaries are contained in F.S. Regs., Part II. and the Staff Manual respectively. Title pages will be prepared in manuscript.

Place	Date Sept.	Hour	Summary of Events and Information	Remarks and references to Appendices
	1.		Lt Wicks & Bus to report in buildings.	
	2.	10.30	O.C. r/Adjt round lines	
	3.		O.C. inspected Sections	
	4.		Lt Mackie attached for duty. Lt Cross in buildings board	
			Swagras of No 1 Section instr Capt Lucas to charges to be returned to Adv. Horse depot. Instructors vice to Sens Capt Lewis to Aboukir	
	5.	4 p.m.	Church parade.	
	6.		O.C. v Adjt to 4 S.M. Rd. Rigging party from 3. S.M. Rd returned with Mount. rifles Reg-	
	7.		Capt Lucas reported from Aboukir. Lt Darling Avc reported to 1st Bde	
	8.		O.C. inspected all Sections	
	10.		S.A.C. moved to Trevews. Capt Lucas a Para.	
	12.		O.C. inspected Section. Rfset from Goreen & Bde Major. 4.30. Church parade with Chaplain Mitchell.	
	13.		Trench wireheads used for all Sections. Lt D Jean's Avc reported	
	14.		Motor Central pointed to Tresrio	
	16.		Capt Bailey R.A.M.C. orr Mr precautions against auture	
	17.		H.E. MK 44 exchanged	
	18.		F G.O.M. Gr Rutles. O.C. arrived with Goreen & Bus	
	19.		Court Martial promulgated. Capt Lucas back from Cairo	
	20.		Capt Wyrtenham reported to assume duties of Adjutant	
	22.		Capt Saunders attached R.A.M.C. G.O.C. Bus called. 6 p.m.	
	23.		Advanced Relief. 48 Sub Park arrived at Tresrio. Short rifles exchanged for Long rifles	
	24.		Ammunition supplied at Corps scale	
	25.		Capt Wells, 6th Lr Eng, Hns.	
	26.		Capt Wyrtenham inspected Std Ha Co. 9 A.M. OC to see SOCRA at 7 p.m.	
	27.		Lt Cross appointed temporary adjutant. Rec'd orders return all Mospielli Comids	
	28.		Surplus Ammunition returned to DAC from Bde Columns	
	30.		1654 horses under Corps	

COMMDG: R. M. Moore LT-COL. DIVL. AMMUNITION COLUMN.

48. CAPT ADJT DIVL. AMMUNITION COLUMN.

121/7435

48th Division

48th Div. Ammn. Col.

Oct. '15

Vol. VII

<u>Confidential</u>

WAR DIARY.

OF

48" (South Mid) Divisional Ammunition Column.

From 1st October 1915 to 31st October 1915.

Volume XV

WAR DIARY
or
INTELLIGENCE SUMMARY.
(Erase heading not required.)

Army Form C. 2118.

Instructions regarding War Diaries and Intelligence Summaries are contained in F. S. Regs., Part II. and the Staff Manual respectively. Title pages will be prepared in manuscript.

Place	Date Oct/16	Hour	Summary of Events and Information	Remarks and references to Appendices
	1.		OC to RA HQ Ono	
	2.		Advanced Section 48 Sub Park. left for Theipval. Concert given to B.A.C. by Recruits. Staff Supply Trapes	
	3.		Section Curuceuses and RE Officer J. O'Neill. Church parade with Col. Thomas. 4.30 p.m. Capt. Hughes am. reported again for duty as acq. polar.	
	4.		OC inspected horses in morning.	
	5.		Capt + OC to RA Hd Qrs.	
	6.		Adjt to RA HQ Qrs.	
	7.		Driving drill for first time in LD horses by OC.	
	8.		Staff Captain arr. re Wedding Party Note re Trains.	
	9.		2nd Lieut Kidd arrived. Thanks for attachment.	
	10.		Church parade Col. Thomas 4.30 p.m.	
	11.		Section all inspected GOC Sir CMC to inspect horses later horses.	
	12.		Driving Drill	
	13.		No 1 horses inspected by VO.	
	14.		No 2 Section inspected by OC. No 3 Section rifles inspected by Officers.	
	16.		Attentials to harness cart to brs. safety officer re extra day relief.	
	17.		No 3 Section horses inspected by VO. 4.30 Church parade by Col. Thomas.	
	18.		Adjt + C RAHQ Qrs + 3rd Pres. Section Tubes Gr. Future ammunition.	
	19.		No 4 Section horses inspected by VO. ADMS Ons. to inspect billets. 4. S.M. Kidd to drain i humble as Offrs.	
	20.		OC + 4 S.M. Kidd began Brunches Classes officers One re hiring of fields for trails. Quartrs. 3rd Lieuds Nott arr'd Norris	
	21.		No 1 Section horses inspected + to Capt. Savage RAMC re Cases.	
	22.		OC inspected Driving Drill + Lts. to RA Hd Qrs.	
	23.		No 2 Section horses inspected	
	24.		Driving Drill Completition Lecture 4. M. Salt, 4 S.M. Kidd.	
	25.		No 3 Section horses inspector	
	26.		OC round lines. Staff Captain. ADS. RA Ons.	
	27.		No 4 Section horses inspected by VO. 2 cars Canadian Ammunition Ary + Bus re Adv. Section (bombs) at Corbie Magazine	
	28.		OC Adjt + Y. Staff Captain to Corbieux. Select ground for B.A.C. Magazine	
	29.		No 1 Section horses inspected by VO. OC + Adjt + 4. S.M. Kidd in action.	
	30.		YA QMG + Staff Captain Ons. re Collecting heavy batteries. 2nd Lieut Norris	
	31.		No 2 Section horses inspected by VO. RE Ons. re Hesitation room. Church parade 3.30 p.m. Lieut + Col. Thomas	

1577 Wt. W.10791/1773 500,000 1/15 D.D. & L. A.D.S.S./Forms/C. 2118.

C.M.Moag LT-COL.
COMDG. 48. DIVL. AMMUNITION COLUMN.

Confidential.

War Diary.

of

48th (S.M.) Divl. Amn. Column.

from 1st. November 1915 — 30th Nov. 1915.

Volume ~~XVI~~ VIII

Army Form C. 2118.

WAR DIARY
or
INTELLIGENCE SUMMARY.
(Erase heading not required.)

Instructions regarding War Diaries and Intelligence Summaries are contained in F. S. Regs., Part II. and the Staff Manual respectively. Title pages will be prepared in manuscript.

Place	Date	Hour	Summary of Events and Information	Remarks and references to Appendices
In the field.	Nov 1st 1915 2nd		O.C. to Bus & Coigneux. Lt Edwards joined.	
	3rd		No 3 Section inspected by V.O. Meeting of Sec. Cmdrs & NCOs re Courtlim	
	4th		Courtmartial Cp.Sadler STARR at Sailly OC & Adjt to Bus. RA Hd Qrs.	
	5th		V.O. inspected No4 Section. OC & Capt Burbidge on leave. Capt Wykeham	
	6th		A.S.C. Wagons inspected by SM of A.S.C. Capt Wykeham sans GO.CRA re Courtmartial re Cp Sad. STARR.	
	7th		V.O. inspected No 1. Section	
	8th		Church parade 3.30 p.m. by Rev Helin.	
	9th		OC to Coigneux to advanced Section.	
	10th		No 2 Section horses inspected	
	11th		OC & Capt Hewitt to Sailly for FGCM on Cp Saddler STARR	
	12th		A.S.M. Broom on leave	
	13th		Adjt to Coigneux	
	14th		No 4 horses inspected by V.O. Lt Col Browne back from leave.	
	15th		Church parade under Chaplain Helin.	
	16th		Capt Harlow on leave in civil life for No 1 horses inspected V.V.O.	
	17th		40 Recess Act-Adjt. During time made for Bde Major	
	18th		Staff Captain ran re 99,000 SAA	
	19th		OC inspected Circus	
	20th		OC to RA Hd Qrs	
	21st		Dinner to NCOs to celebrate 1st anniversary of 46 D.A.C.	
	22nd		Mr. Issue of Rum. Church parade 6 p.m. Chaplain Thomas.	
	23rd		No 3 section route marched. No 4 Hd Qrs horses inspected V.V.O. 4 5 Battery 36 Division around Vierres Evacuants 2 changing arms	
	24th		Courtmartial Pte J. Brown at 3rd Bde Hd Qrs	
			Section 36 B.A.C. under Lt Smith attached.	

1577 Wt.W10791/1773 500,000 1/15 D. D. & L. A.D.S.S./Forms/C. 2118.

Army Form C. 2118.

WAR DIARY
or
INTELLIGENCE SUMMARY.
(Erase heading not required.)

Instructions regarding War Diaries and Intelligence Summaries are contained in F. S. Regs., Part II. and the Staff Manual respectively. Title pages will be prepared in manuscript.

Place	Date	Hour	Summary of Events and Information	Remarks and references to Appendices
In the Field	November 1915	25	Promulgation of Ct. martial at St. Eton. No 4 Section refitted/reinforced. V.O. inspected No 1 horses	
		26	All weary horses segregated in field. A.D.V.S. own in afternoon. No 1 Section rout-marched. Capt Lipheban others.	
		27	Pte C.R.A. at Adv. Section. B.S.M. Brown back from leave.	
		28	Lt. Edwards to Odn. Sectin i/c.	
		29	13 horses evacuated for mange. Close billeting reconnaissance. Cantien others.	
		30	Section 4 V.O. and horse in am after up to Borcette kange.	

L. W. Moore
Lt. Col.
COMMD 48th DIVL. AMMUNITION COLUMN.

4ºᵗᵉ Dive Cavan. F. Col.

Dec / Vol IX

Army Form C. 2118.

WAR DIARY
or
INTELLIGENCE SUMMARY.
(Erase heading not required.)

Instructions regarding War Diaries and Intelligence Summaries are contained in F. S. Regs., Part II. and the Staff Manual respectively. Title pages will be prepared in manuscript.

Place	Date	Hour	Summary of Events and Information	Remarks and references to Appendices
In the field	1 Dec /15		O.C. to Advanced section. Staff Captain R.A. Inspected billets.	
	2 "	"	R.E. Officer came over re supplying material for repair of billets.	
	3 "	"	Inspection: horses moved into new field. 14 men Reinforcement R.A. came over re billeting. Bde for night in THIEVRES.	
			26 reinforcement arrived.	
	5 "	"	Vet Off. inspected horses. Six men pleuran inspected horse lines. Capt Wyndham returned from leave	
	6 "	"	O.C. went round all sections.	
	7 "	"	Ord: march for Arty Action. O.C. to COIGNEUX. C.R.E. D.A.A.Q.M.G. & Staff Capt. R.A. came over re billeting scheme.	
	8 "	"		
	9 "	"	O.C. went round all sections.	
	10 "	"	Adj. to COIGNEUX. Officers & NCOs attend lecture on gas at COUIN.	
	11 "	"	1st CPO S.G. went on leave.	
	12 "	"	Church Parade at 6 p.m.	
	13 "	"	O.C. & Adj to BdS. H.Q & Aske D.A.D.O.S. (Asst Commdant inspected all horses of A.C.). 1st PARKER 30 B.A.C. arrived for instruction.	
	14 "	"	O.C. went round all sections.	
	15 "	"	O.C. arranges for piquets & had village fire engine put in order, Adj to Advanced section. A.P.M. × D.A.Q.M.G. came over re road control.	
	16 "	"	O.C. went round section. Adj to LOUVANCOURT re fodder & lamps. 149 Bde came back to billet for night	
	17 "	"	A.B. Patterson 149 Bde left THIEVRES.	
	18 "	"	Vet Off. inspected 2nd sec horses. C. O Battn. 149 Bde came into billet	

H. Wyndham
CAPT., ADJT.
48th DIVL. AMMUNITION COLUMN.

Army Form C. 2118.

WAR DIARY
INTELLIGENCE SUMMARY.
(Erase heading not required.)

Place	Date	Hour	Summary of Events and Information	Remarks and references to Appendices
In the Field	19 Dec 15		Ch. Parade 6 pm. G.O.C. came over.	
	20 "		Route March for 3rd Sec. Adj to BAYENCOURT & Reservation R.A. Then also to COIGNEUX, R. Omitica	
	21 "		A.V.C. to R. over Vet Intlus. Vis Lt Pick-Jones.	
	22 "		O.C. went round all returns	
			Adj to COIGNEUX. Ammunt Return.	
	23 "		O.C. to Hd Qrs R.A.	
	25 "		Church Parade 11. am	
	26 "		Adj to F.G.C.M. on Gr PILLEY at BAYENCOURT	
	27 "		C.O went round sections. Bombs dropped by German Aeroplane near MAILLY. Vet Off inspected horses of 1st Sec. Ammunition Train forced by ORC from Enthused trans. Motor lorries.	
	29 "		Adj to BUS - COIGNEUX. C.O to HEBUTERNE. Sentence of F.G.C.M. promulgated on Gr PILLEY.	
	31st "		O.C. inspected sections - Adj to COIGNEUX.	

[Signature] Wyndham
CAPT., ADJT.
48th DIVL. AMMUNITION COLUMN.

Confidential.

War Diary

of

48" Divisional Ammunition Column.

from 1st January to 31st January 1916.

Volume ~~XVII~~ X

Army Form C. 2118.

WAR DIARY
or
INTELLIGENCE SUMMARY.
(Erase heading not required.)

Instructions regarding War Diaries and Intelligence Summaries are contained in F. S. Regs., Part II. and the Staff Manual respectively. Title pages will be prepared in manuscript.

Place	Date	Hour	Summary of Events and Information	Remarks and references to Appendices
In the field	1st Jan/16		O.C. went round Sections. Adj. to Corps Am. Park.	
	2nd "		Vet. Off inspected horses of 3rd Sec. Church Parade 6pm. G.O.C. 40 Div came.	
	3rd "		Inspection of 3rd Sec. w. Drill order.	
	4 "		50 men left Town 8p.m. 5 minds in Trenches. Lecture by Capt Birkett on Cliff Fire.	
	5 "		Bde. Insp. R.A. Cmme. sent re Ammunition.	
	6 "		40 men sent to DOULLENS Railhead. New 4.5 guns. Vet inspection of 4th Sec horses.	
	7 "		2nd Sec. inspected for trenches. Party left 12 noon 8 guns in trenches.	
	8 "		Adj. to COIGNEUX. Vet inspection of 2nd Sec horses.	
	9 "		Ch. Parade 6 pm. Bishop of B'ham gave address. G.O.C. came.	
	10 "		O.C. inspected all saddlery. Munition workers interviewed by inspector.	
	11 "		Vet Inspection of 4th Sec horses.	
	12 "		O.C. Adj. to HQ Am. Park. All 5" How Amn. returned to D.A.C. from Batteries. Am. Col.	
	13 "		40 men sent to DOULLENS to load up 5" How guns. 61 reinforcements came.	
	14 "		General Officer A.D.V.S. inspected all horses 10.30 a.m. Vet inspection of 4th horses.	
	15 "		O.C. & Adj. HUMISTON & met Vet Sec N (Claude's horse)	
	16 "		O.C. & HQ R.A. Church Parade 6 pm. Vet Inspection No 3 Sec horses.	
	17 "		A.D.O.S. VII Corps Came sent re harness stores.	
	18 "		O.C. & Adjt. Sec. COIGNEUX. A.D.O.S. VII Corps. Horse forage store at COIGNEUX. Branch Stn	
	19 "		Ammunition for THIEPVAL.	
	" "		Adj. & Col. 145 Adj. re ambce. Guides. 58 men sent 8 guns in trenches.	
	21 "		71 men sent to DOULLENS for remounts.	
	22 "		Adj. to Advanced Section COIGNEUX.	

WAR DIARY
or
INTELLIGENCE SUMMARY.
(Erase heading not required.)

Army Form C. 2118.

Instructions regarding War Diaries and Intelligence Summaries are contained in F. S. Regs., Part II. and the Staff Manual respectively. Title pages will be prepared in manuscript.

Place	Date	Hour	Summary of Events and Information	Remarks and references to Appendices
In the Field	23rd Jan 16		Ch. Parade 6 p.m.	
	24		Carting bricks from DOULLENS for R.A.	
	25		A.T.3 Pte horses inspected. S. Captain R.A. present in afternoon.	
	26		Res. H.Q. 1, 2 & 3 inspected in full order. 21 reinforcements issued. Gas alarm 7.30 p.m.	
	27		Inspection of A.T. horses & harness. Kit inspection A.T. horses 2 p.m. A.T. 1 & 3 Coy inspected	
	28		for boots & clothing.	
	29		Gas reported coming over 7 a.m.	
	30		Adv: R-HUS - AUTHIE & more of Othe. Church Parade 6 p.m.	
	31		Adv: RAUTHIE in billets.	

[signature] Wykeham
CAPT., ADJT.
49th DIVL. AMMUNITION COLUMN.

Confidential

WAR DIARY.
OF
48th DIVISIONAL AMMUNITION COLUMN

From 1st to 29th February 1916.

Volume ~~XX~~. XI

Army Form C. 2118.

WAR DIARY
or
INTELLIGENCE SUMMARY.
(Erase heading not required.)

Instructions regarding War Diaries and Intelligence Summaries are contained in F. S. Regs., Part II. and the Staff Manual respectively. Title pages will be prepared in manuscript.

Place	Date	Hour	Summary of Events and Information	Remarks and references to Appendices
In the field	1st Feb 1916		O.C. – Adj to AUTHIE re billeting of DAC.	
	2		O.C. to AUTHIE re horse standings etc.	
	3		Moved Garrison Quartermasters Stores to AUTHIE	
	4		O.C. – Adj to AUTHIE. Bomb stow moved over – all stores	
	5		DAC moved to AUTHIE starting at 9 a.m. Move complete by 10.15 a.m. All horses in the open	
	6		O.C. went round all horse lines. G.O.C. ordered horse standings	
	7		Adj to BUS to see Ordnance Officer. Staff Capt R.A. came over the matter.	
	8		O.C. & Adj to COIGNEUX Adv. Cav. – 1 R.A. & 4 Inf Officers collected from LOUVENCOURT	
	9		O.C. to COULINCAMPS re provisioning F.G.C.M. – 7 R.A. Officers arrived 6 p.m., 5 wagons of Grindle sent to 37th Division.	
	10		O.C. inspected billets in the morning, & all rifles in the afternoon –	
	11		3 Tees moved into horse standings vacated by 4th Glosters Regt.	
	12		O.C. & Adj to THIEVRES re its billets re event of a move back there. Vet inspection of 1st Tee horses –	
	13		Lt Col. G.B. Browne went on leave & Capt Hutchinson left in charge. 1st See took over horse standings vacated by 4 R. Berks Transport.	
	14		Received orders at 11 p.m. to move to THIEVRES on 16 inst.	
	15		Sec Coms to THIEVRES re billets, 141 Remounts collected from MONDICOURT, 24 of these for DAC.	
	16		10 a.m. DAC moved to THIEVRES.	
	17		Adj to BUS to see claims officer re clauns in THIEVRES –	
	19		Adj to AUTHIE re supplies - Vet Inspec horses 10.3 Sec 2 p.m.	
	20		C.L Parade 6 p.m. in Recreation Rm	
	21		Vet Inspec 1st & Sec – HQ horses at 2 p.m.	

Army Form C. 2118.

WAR DIARY
or
INTELLIGENCE SUMMARY.
(Erase heading not required.)

Instructions regarding War Diaries and Intelligence Summaries are contained in F. S. Regs., Part II. and the Staff Manual respectively. Title pages will be prepared in manuscript.

Place	Date	Hour	Summary of Events and Information	Remarks and references to Appendices
In the field	22 Feb '16		Lt Col (P.B. Browne) returned from leave. Snow fell during day. Bri Park came.	
	23"		O.C. Watford sections. Claims officer over to LAVILETTES.	
	24"		Marching drill & physical exercises for 2 & 3 sections. Vet Inspn N°7 sec.	
	25"		Roads very bad. 46 Ted Park brought up - (scamped) their estab. of ammunition at 6 p.m.	
	26"		Received intim that 3rd Army traffic into no force.	
	27"		30 G.S. wagons sent to RAILHEAD at 3.30 a.m. 8 days supplies on account of 3rd Army traffic intro. Dep: Chief: Came to French - Brig Gen H.D.O.WARD Comdk 48 div R.A. over.	
	28"		30 G.S. wagons sent as yesterday - Enquiry held into LAVILETTES claims.	
	29"		30 G.S. wagons as yesterday. Capt. G.B. LUCAS LUCAS attached to the F.A. Bde (Hers).	

Wykehan
CAPT., ADJT.
48th DIVL. AMMUNITION COLUMN.

Confidential
War Diary
of
48th (South Midland)
Divisional Ammunition Column.
R.F.A.
from 1st March 1916 to 31st March 1916.

Volume ~~XX~~ XII

WAR DIARY
INTELLIGENCE SUMMARY

Army Form C. 2118.

Place	Date	Hour	Summary of Events and Information	Remarks and references to Appendices
In the field	1st March		30 G.S. wagons sent to Railhead to draw supplies. Vet Officer inspected sick horses.	
	2nd		O.C. went round all sections.	
	3rd		114 Heavy Battery came to THIEVRES for night. O.C. 46th Divl Supply Col came to billets.	
	4th		C.O. took Lieut Andrews re F.G.C.M. on Corp DEAVES. Billeting officer of 46 Supply Col over.	
	5th		48th Divl Supply Col. came in to billet. 1 S.A.A. wagon received from 46 Divl Train.	
	6th		O.C. inspected No 3 sec in full order.	
	7th		Officer rode 10 am. Adj. & Adjt Vet See COIGNEUX - RE store - Capt Lucas Lucas wounded.	
	8th		O.C. & R.A.H.Q. F.G.C.M. on Cpl DEAVES at DAC. H.Q.	
	9th		Brig Genl H.D.O. WARD inspected horses of DAC at 3.15 pm.	
	10th		12 G.S. wagons to LOCH BOX road to telephone poles H/s leslie Grierstock & Bay sent to 3rd Bde.	
	11th		2 lorries came for 16th Seige Battn. Adjt to See claims officer R.E.	
	12th		4 comn Sub Lt Wordicourt for steel rods. Church parade under Chaplain Mitchell. Sir Andrews present.	
	13th		O.C. to Helvetine. Gunner Petty killed at Helvetine.	
	14th		Funeral of Gunner Petty at Helvetine. Chaplain Le Smith officiated. O.C. to R.A.H.Q. Div.	
	15th		Adjutant and Lt Edwards visited T.M. batteries at Helvetine.	
	16th		O.C. to R.A. Hd Qrs	
	17th		O.C. round all sections.	
	18th		Lt Parker 95 T.M. Batty. Adjt C 3rd Army T.M. School. 3,000 rds. 18 pdr. sent up.	
	19th		Church Parade 6pm by Chaplain Mitchell.	
	20th		Offrs received that Sr C Lucas Arthurs 26 W.ach. Odrs rec'd for 28 teams to be found daily for A.S.C. Supply work.	
	21st		O.C + Adjt to Arthurs re billets. Adjt to Bus R.A. Hd Qrs.	
	22nd		O.C + Adjt to Arthurs re billets for horses.	
	23rd		Sedn Commando to Arthurs to arrange billets etc.	
	26th		Began to move supplies, stores, Column etc.	

Army Form C. 2118.

WAR DIARY
or
INTELLIGENCE SUMMARY.
(Erase heading not required.)

Instructions regarding War Diaries and Intelligence Summaries are contained in F. S. Regs., Part II. and the Staff Manual respectively. Title pages will be prepared in manuscript.

Place	Date	Hour	Summary of Events and Information	Remarks and references to Appendices
In the Field	27 March 16		531 NCOs & Men & 9 officers min. forwards for RA. arrived at THIEVRES. 6 p.m. Staff Captain. arr. 9.30pm	
	28	"	re. MT & MD charges & re. prin. for No.1 Section. Capt Wykeham went on leave.	
	29	"	OC. to AUTHIE + to BARTON re. ammunition. Belonged 11 AD for 15 LD. W.E.P.S.C. Gunners collected Kits to AUTHIE	
	30	"	4th section split up among No 1 & 3 Sections. OC. to KRAthi Gs. Saw Gd. ERA. re Capt Wykeham PDG as Staff Captain. RA.	
	31	"	28 items for A.S.C. supply work arranged. OC. WULELIE 169 Am. Col. re Shirrins, 56 min forceness, Gun. 3rd line arrived	
			Am. Col. 169 Bde. around Thievres. Staff Captain called 11. min. OC. inspected No.1 Section in afternoon 2/Lt MICHOUS	
			to Y.48. TM Battery	

C. W. Moore
LT.-COL.
COMMD. 48th DIVL. AMMUNITION COLUMN.

Vol XIII
48.

CONFIDENTIAL
War Diary.

Unit.   Divisional Ammunition Column.

Brigade.   —

Division.   Forty-eighth.

Mobilization Centre. }   Chelmsford.

Temporary War Station. }   —

Stations since occupied subsequent to Mobilization. }   —

WAR DIARY or INTELLIGENCE SUMMARY

Army Form C. 2118.

Place	Date	Hour	Summary of Events and Information	Remarks and references to Appendices
Rue File Ferla	1 April 1916		2/Lt NICHOLS attached Y.T.M. Battery. OC to THIEVRES to arrange Am. Supply with OC 169 Am. Col.	
	2 April 1916	do	Lieut Ward called 9.45. OC inspected billets. DAAQMG & Staff Captain RA. arr. re Nos 1 & 3 Sections moving	
	3rd do	do	No 1 Section moved to west Area. OC to Jarnechon re patrol lines & to 48 Sub Park re Empty Cases	
	4th do	do	Nov Stores divided between Nos 1, 2 & 3 Sections. OC inspected Sun 3 Stores. OC to DADOS. & to THIEVRES re compensation claims	
	5th do	do	OC inspected HdQrs & No 2 Section. Motor lorry to Halatine at night	
	6th do	do	ADVS. inspected 27 HD horses	
	7th do	do	Qms TURNER & SERGT COCKRAM horse & wheelers furlough. 27 HD horses sent to 32nd & 7th Divisions. Capt Wykeham back from leave	
	8th do	do	OC attended Conference. Genl Fanshawe Sam Brownes.	
	9th do	do	Capt WYKEHAM to HdQrs 6th Div.	
	10th do	do	DAAQMG over in morning. OC inspected No 3 Section in afternoon	
	11th do	do	ADVS over re remounts. 1 HD horse sent to Vet Hon. Sir OC to conference at 11am	
	12th do	do	Capt LEA to Bde HQ. Capt WYKEHAM over re Officers. ADVS inspects 9 HD horses	
	13th do	do	2/Lt BLAND reports from 1st Bde & 2/Lt LYNES from 2nd Bde for attachment	
	14th do	do	ADVS. inspected N.D horses to be transferred. OC to conference. 2/Lt KANNAM reports from 3rd Bde for attachment. 35 HD horses	
	15th do	do	OC inspects clothing re transfer	
	16th do	do	VO inspects No 1 Sec horses. Sgt RAWBONE & No 1 Sec. 2/Lt MICHALLS from 4th Bde for attachment (transferred to others) 21 HD horses	
	17th do	do	OC inspects Arms & clothing No 1 Sec. 2/Lt GEDYE replaces 2/Lt BLAND from 1st Bde	
	18th do	do	Capt MARSHALL attached for instruction. C.O.s Conference. 2/Lt EDWARDS takes charge of No 3 Sec. 2/Lt JUCKES attached to No 3	
	19th do	do	VO inspects No 2 Sec horses. Officers & NCOs Reconnoitre and ride	
	20th do	do	ADVS inspects 12 HD horses transferred to T.M.B. 38 mules arrive from base	
	21st do	do	Capt HOPKINS & TM Battery. 2/Lt NICHALLS in charge No 2 Sec ADVS inspects 10 horses (1 D) transferred to HAC Church Parade 10.30am	
	22nd do	do	O.C. inspects Tarma of No 2 Sec. No 3 Sec Horse Lines moved.	
	23rd do	do	Ammunition issuing Pam Home (Army Si Gas HQ.	
	24th do	do	Capt LUCAS LUCAS reports for duty. 2/Lt MICHALLS returning to 4 Bde. Officer ride 6 p.m.	
	25th do	do	Capt LUCAS LUCAS takes command of No 2 Sec. OC inspects Advance Section	
	26th do	do	2/Lt MATHIESON reports from Base. Driving drill No 1 & 2 Section. Officers ride 6 pm	
	27th do	do	Filtered tanks filled Advance Section	
	28th do	do	2/Lt ASSINDER on leave	
	29th do	do	164 LD Remounts in. V.O. inspects No 1 Section. (Sort of Enquiry re fire 11.15am Driving drill	
	30th do	do	OC inspected HdQrs & No 2 Section. Church parade 6 pm under Chaplain BROWN	

Signed 48th Divl. Ammunition Column.

WAR DIARY
or
INTELLIGENCE SUMMARY.
(Erase heading not required.)

Army Form C. 2118.

Place	Date	Hour	Summary of Events and Information	Remarks and references to Appendices
In Field	Feb 1st 1916		Attached Mules Y & M Batters. OC to Theatre. O Gp.a of Sp. AA Supply with OC 114 Brigade	
	2nd do		Funeral. CMR G45. OC inspects No 1. Dr.S. DR'S of Sept Collar. R.A. M.C. to No 1's Station at O.K.S.	
	3rd do		No 1 Section went to new area. OC to Thurcher to inspect lines & Lines Bn. Pte Q. Ralph, CAMC	
	4th do		Now Slaughterer retained Mules 1 & 3 Sections. OC on relief from 5 lines OC & OHDOS to B3 DH330 to Compensation claims	
	5th do		OC inspects HR(v) & No 3 section, instructions & Instructions at 14Cdn	
	6th do			
	7th do		ADVS inspects 27 HD horses SDN 6 c 32, 7 Jewelry. Officer wounded Shrady C Start C or 7 3rd Bn	
	8th do		QM's 7 Furnace Spiritual Home re events. for trough. 27 HD horses SN 16 32, 17 Pervisions. C.O Inspection Instruction.	
	9th do		O.C. attending Conference. General Frankfurt - Gen W Thomas.	
	10th do		Captain White to HQ 46 Brigade inspected No 3 Section in advance.	
	11th do		Dept.V.S. OC in Morning. OC Inspected No 3 Section in afternoon.	
	12th do		ADVS men in remounts. 1 HD horse sent to Vet Div OC & conference at 6am.	
	13th do		Capt LEA to Brig HQ. Capt NYKEHAM on m Officer. ADVS inspects 9 HD horses 5 21st Bde, H/Lt ASSINDER adjutant	
	14th do		2/Lt BLAND reports to HD from 18th Bde & 3HD LINES from 2nd Bde for attachment	
	15th do		ADVS inspects H D horses to be transferred. OC to conference. Lt HANNAM reports from 3rd Bde for attachment 35 HD horses	
	16th do		OC inspects clothing & boots N 3 Section. VO Inspects No 3 Section. (Transferred to other Units)	
	17th do		VO inspects No 1 Sec horses. S/E RAWSONE attac on formation Engagement. H/Lt MICHAELS from 4th Bde for attachment 21 HD horses	
	18th do		OC Inspects teams relieving No 1 Sec. H/Lt GEDGE replaces H/Lt BLAND from 18th Bde. 2/Lt JONES from 3rd Lines, Driving drill 9am, Church parade	
	19th do		Capt MARSHALL attached for instruction. C.O. to Conference. H/Lt EDWARDS taken charge of No 3 Sec. H/Lt JONES attacked to No 3	
	20th do		VO Inspects No 2 Sec horses. Officers & NCO's recommence route	
	21st do		ADVS inspects 12 HD horses transferred to HQ. 38 mules arrive from here	
	22nd do		Capt HOPKINS 6 TM battery H/Lt MICHAELS in charge No 2 Sec. ADVS inspects 12 horses (14 D) transferred to 3 ASC. Church	
	23rd do		OC inspects team of No 3 Sec. No 3 Sec horses been moved. Parade 10.30am	
	24th do		Communion Service 9am. Horse flow at Brig HQ	
	25th do		Capt LUCAS LUCAS reports for duty. H/Lt NICHAELS returns to 4th Bde. Officers ride 6pm.	
	26th do		Capt LUCAS LUCAS attached for duty w/ No 2 Sec. OC inspects advance section	
	27th do		H/Lt MATHISSON reports from 4th Bde.	
	28th do		Returned bomb shell killed Advance section officers ride 6pm.	
	29th do		21 HD mules on leave. VO inspects No 1 Section. Driving drill N 1 & 2 section. Officers ride 6pm. (out of infantry) & fire 10am. Driving drill	
	30th do do		154 L.D. Remounts in. Church parade 6 Am Aux'y, Chaplain Beven.	

D.M. Arthur

Vol 14

War Diary

48th (South Midland)
Divisional Ammunition Column. R.F.A.

May 1916.

Volume ~~XVIII~~

WAR DIARY
or
INTELLIGENCE SUMMARY

Army Form C. 2118.

Place	Date	Hour	Summary of Events and Information	Remarks and references to Appendices
In the field	1st May 1916		ADMS inspects 2B HD horses the transferred to other units. Also two new batteries left by motor lorry at 11 pm	
	2		O.C. visits gun position with G.O.C.R.A. Staff Captain over to Corries	
	3		Capt. SPEAR – 2/Lt BASSETT, MATTHEWS, HUSTLER & FLOWERS report. O.C. inspect horses of 4" Batty. 4 = S.M. B RFA.	
	4			
	5		13 HD handed over to 30th Bde squadron 9 A.M. O.C. to COVIN	
	6		Capt. LUCAS on leave. ADVS inspect 22 LD horses to go a HD	
	7		Church parade 10 AM. Capt. BROWN. 15 LD horses to other units	
	8		2/Lt EDWARDS to CANVAS timing 12 noon 2 w/o D.Batt., GOCRA inspects horses 5.30 pm	
	9		2/Lt APPINDER reports from leave. No 3 Section horses return to original lines & are inspected by VO.	
	10		VO inspects No 1 Section horses. Adjut. 2/Lt JAMESON x grazing	
	11		O.C. to COVIN x home. 19 horses returned to Dukmnnst.	
	12		O.C. inspects No 2 section. 2/Lt EDWARDS x 2/Lt MILKINS return. Details of oxygen etc received	
	13		O.C. on leave. Capt. BURBIDGE takes command. DAG.	
	14		Church parade 10.30 am. Capt. BROWN returns, 2/Lt LEDGER x 2/Lt phu. DUBUAC.	
	15		Capt. SAUNDERS x 2/Lt MOTTRAM from u/Bde. Bde Am Col. obtained. 1 x 3 Section Dac. Capt. THORNS attacked	
	16		Capt. WYKEHAM over x new establishment. 30 HD handed over 2/2 by 2/Lt Section BQM BROWN returns from leave	
	17		101 LD horses transferred to Batteries by u/Bde. Horses received from ASP. Capt LANDER transferred to 241 Bde	
	18		Major LATTY reports for duty. 241 BU x takes command of DAC	
	19		14 horses received from u/Bde units & 236 horses from 31 Bde Am Col.	
	20		4 Section Lines moved to new standings, vaccines started.	
	21		Church parade 10.30 am. Suspect mules to join No 4	
	22		2/Lt EDWARD OR BURN on leave. Inspects new horse lines. 2 horse HD handed out. 5 mules received from 243 Bde	
	23		2 Riders received from WARLOY 36 LD horses received from DV.H.E VILLERS. O.C. inspects No 1 x still rides	
	24		O.C. inspects mules of No 1 & 2 Section. 26 LD horses handed over to 21 Div. O.C. inspects No 3 Batty. in still order	
	25		BSM COCKRAM reports to BQMS for B.Echelon 6 horses handed over to 242 Bde. B.QM. BURBIDGE a'sumed 9 Am	
	26		Capt HEWITT x 2/Lt LINET on leave returned from 241 Bde to Brigade 2	
	27		Check parade 9.30 am. Change of No 3 2nd HD horses handed over. 468s and 2 7.8 mm 6/11	
	28		Capt SPEARE in command of No 3 Section	
	29		10 HD horses handed over to Siv. Tran. (B) 2/Lt AMBULANCE (1). 5 Group (1). O.C. inspects No 3 Sec.	
	30		Capt. LEDGER S/ LEDGER	
	31		8 AC inspected in marching order by G.O. & HD to 22nd HAG. O.C. inspects No 3 See Major LATTY to ENGLAND.	

Lieut. Adjt.

War Diary.

48th (South Midland) Divisional Ammunition Column.

June 1916.

Volume ~~XIX~~

Army Form C. 2118.

WAR DIARY or INTELLIGENCE SUMMARY

(Erase heading not required.)

Instructions regarding War Diaries and Intelligence Summaries are contained in F. S. Regs., Part II. and the Staff Manual respectively. Title Pages will be prepared in manuscript.

Place	Date	Hour	Summary of Events and Information	Remarks and references to Appendices
In the field	June 1/16		28 Riders received from rail head distributed to the units	
	2		GOC RA inspects BAC. Left half marching order 9.30 a.m. 2/Lt DAVEY & Lt HASSALL report from 242 Bde 2/Lt SINDER sick/post WAC (Appx B)	
	3		V.O. inspects horses of all sections 2/Lt STAINTON & MATHIESON to leave	
	4		Capt BURBIDGE departs as artillery officer. 2/Lt PYKE & SMITH report from base. CO to HQ 2 more	
	5		No 1 Sec & No 2 LEDGER, No 2 Section to COIGNEUX Capt ANDERSON reports to unit	
	6		Capt ANDERSON W/O command No.1 Section	
	7		No 2 Sec moved to 240 Bde A ET COURT reports from 240 Bde to proceed to No 2 section 1st Wagon 43 batteries with ammunition	
	8		Lieut N. & C. to COIGNEUX OC to court martial Sgt. H.R.MANTON W/C to No 4 Section	
	9		OC BAC to 242 Bde No 4 Section	
	10		6½ LD + 22 mules received from railhead	
	11		OC inspects No 1 & 2 Section, 240 mm TM ammunition moved at dump	
	12		GOC RA inspects officer OC inspects No 1 Section	
	13		2/Lt MATHIESON & STAYNTON report from base 2 TM bombs to HEBUTERNE	
	14		Capt CROCKROAD reports sick, attached 2 TM bombs to HEBUTERNE	
	15		18 pr Wagons attached to 29th Division	
	16		10 mules ex light section for rec'd 2 TM ammunition to HEBUTERNE	
	17		Church parade & LEDGER 9.20 am All gun positions filled up at PUISIEUX Capt HEWITT in charge. CO to court martial. 2/Lt SMITH reports to 241 Brigade	
	18		240 Mortar with ammunition sent to - sect OC HEBUTERNE & NORTH ZONE (less 4/5 LR)	
	19		122 Horses 11 mules arrived from base (10 mules for SPC)	
	20		French Killed 1 mule at station, 309 rounds 18 pr ammunition sent to Puisieux. Capt to court martial Cap't & Pointer	
	21		2/Lts MATHIESON & PYKE & RHODES destroyed by fire B/ HAMMOND killed 4 F. made half 5 bygetle in guide to	
	22		Some driver & rec'ty by HAMMOND loss of South pr. items built by no section Off. 5 Fred. point 21 ammunition supply	
	23		2 gun drivers now mules wounded lent No.1 Bombardment	
	24		Church parade No. LEDGER & COIGNEUX OC inspects No 4 section	
	25		OC to 243 Battery	
	26		23 min ambulance to 241 Bde + 25 to 243 Bde OC Battery	
	27		OC inspects No 1 & 2 section 10 rounds 240 m ammunition	
	28		Lieut RHODES reports from base No. 4 ammunition sent up to trenches	
	29		15 rounds 240 m TM ammunition arrived fr. 75 Battery	
	30		Rec'd up to trenches. Section Special 75 ammunition convoy.	

G.G.Reynolds
Lieut Adjt.
45th DIVL. AMMUNITION COLUMN.

WAR DIARY.
July, 1916.

48th S.M. DIVISIONAL AMMUNITION COLUMN.
R.F.A.

Volume XX

HEADQUARTERS,
48th (S. M.) DIVISIONAL
AMMUNITION COLUMN.

No ....
Date ....5.8.16.

WAR DIARY or INTELLIGENCE SUMMARY

Army Form C. 2118.

HEADQUARTERS,
48th (S.M.) DIVISIONAL
AMMUNITION COLUMN.

No. ....
Date ......7/2/16...........

Place	Date	Hour	Summary of Events and Information	Remarks and references to Appendices
In the field	1st Feb 1916		Lieut. S.H. RHODES reports at 2.42 B.M. 4.9.	
	2		No 3 Section S.A.A. wagons 2/Lt COLLINS in charge report to MAILLY MAILLETT. Embarkation in plain	
	3		2/Lt COLLINS returns to SS LEDGER with S.A.A. wagons. Guns from H.Q. & prevented attack by enemy	
	4		Capt. HEWITT & 3rd Section 16 pdr wagons returns to SS LEDGER. Remount (rider 12 mules) from FARIFEUILLON	
	5		French ammunition withdrawn from gun positions. 75 battery leaves. New wagons repair section	
	6		O.C. to DOULLENS. French ammunition withdrawn	
	7		31st Division dumps at BUS taken over by 3/4 D.A.C. s/Lt HASSALL in charge	
	8		Captured photos to BUSTILLEN up dumps O.C. to BUS. 4016 EDN 6 p.m. Emplacement moving enemy	
	9		O.C. returns at BUS O.C. inspects No. 1 + 3 + 4 Section	
	10		O.C. to EMPLETON + gun range St CONWAY + 3/Lt RUSHTON RWD Section + RUSTON N.P. + BOND Tt. report from leave	
	11		2/Lt BOND posted RN? Section to Mt interim	
	12		No 2 Section S.A.A. wagons to BOUZINCOURT with 143 Bde st TAUNTON in charge	
	13		No.1 ?pei D.A.C. moved O.C. inspects 1 + 3 Section	
	14		Remounts of 9 A.V. wagon SWARLOY Capt. SMITH CARRINGTON in charge	
	15		Coloured parcel JILDGER 9.30 am Capt. BROWN. Part B JAA Section 36 9th SAA reports for attachment. Hells new Horses	
	16		Captain + Supt. No1 BAG O.C. inspects	
	17		V.O. + Adjutant to return. N.Eich animals Dumps at BUS closed by Senior. 10 horses LD. + 10 mules from base	
	18		Remounts of 36 BAG. 36.9 BAG arrive at SS LEDGER	
	19		Colonel + Adjutant JSCSRAG. Nea + ammunition Dump taken over by 36.5 RC	
	20		D.A.G. to BOUZINCOURT. remarks No6 Section. Dump at TREB RLOY. Column moves off at 10 am.	
	21		O.C. visits Sections new home for No.3 Section. Dump at BOUZINCOURT interline	
	22		O.C. inspects horses + returns. O.C. to WARLOY Congratulation Messages to Sections from O.C. + Section	
	23		O.C. to Bulla positions. Adjutant to FORCEVILLE + return Cm. from Quim? No4 Section	
	24		O.C. inspects No. 4 Section. Inspect returning to position from 1001 + 1.2 Section taken to BOUZINCOURT	
	25		2/Lt. SANSFELD reports. law + inspection from HASSALL from No 1002 + 3rd 2 section	
	26		B.Dm. MADDEN reports from leave 5th section.	
	27		BOUZIRCOURT hill through.	
	28		DAC. moves to AMPLIER at 10 am H.Q. missing 1.30 p.m. 1+4 Section 1 pm	
	29		DAC to ST OUEN to meet M? in advance + meet staff Captain Mc Innes at 5 pm + Section in afternoon 3 Lee tech wagons	
	30		1. 2 + 3 sections to H.Q. in time arrived (to m 39.30)	
	31			

E.C. Marshly?
Lieut.
ADAC.

48th DIVL. AMMUNITION COLUMN

48th (South Midland) Divisional Artillery.

48th DIVISIONAL AMMUNITION COLUMN R.F.A.

AUGUST 1916

48th (South Midland)
Divisional Ammunition Column.
R.F.A.

Army Form C. 2118.

HEADQUARTERS,
48th (S. M.) DIVISIONAL
AMMUNITION COLUMN.
No. Volume 1.
Date AUGUST 1916

WAR DIARY
INTELLIGENCE SUMMARY.
(Erase heading not required.)

Instructions regarding War Diaries and Intelligence Summaries are contained in F. S. Regs, Part II. and the Staff Manual respectively. Title pages will be prepared in manuscript.

Place	Date	Hour	Summary of Events and Information	Remarks and references to Appendices
In Field	1 Aug 1916		Camp inspected by C.R.A.	
	2		2/Lt STANSFELD reports to 242 Brigade. 2/Lt HASALL transferred to 3rd Section S.A.C.	
	3		12 men to 242 Brigade. Divisional band plays in camp.	
	4		2/Lt MATTHEWS reports to 240 Brigade for duty. Curious it-camp	
	5		2/Lt (Temp Capt) BROOKTAYLOR + nine reinforcements report from base	
	6		(Church parade 10 a.m. under Padre McNULTY. Divisional band plays in camp in afternoon	
	7		B.S.M. MADDEN reports for duty to 242 Brigade	
	8		Capt BROOK TAYLOR reports to 240 Brigade	
	9		240 & Divisional artillery to AMPLIER.	
	10		Adjutant to BOUZINCOURT with Op Captain. Court martial at S.A.C. H.Q. Lt Col BROWNE president.	
	11		Brigade leaves AMPLIER. 1 Sub section B section ~ No 1 section to BOUZINCOURT	
	12		Remainder of DAC leaves AMPLIER. 2 + 3 section to BOUZINCOURT. Remainder of Brigade to VARENNES. One letter on wagon commune supply of ammunition rec'd & battery position. (from 12th division)	
	13		2/Lt TAYNTON in charge of No 3 Section. O.C. b Battery position	
	14		Capt HEWITT to England. Lt PYKE to No 2 section. 2/Lt MORRIS reports from base. No 2 bives moved BOUZINCOURT shelled	
	15		O.C. b Battery. No 3 Section bive moved	
	16		trial 2.13 from Trench Mortar Battery Adjutant to battery	
	17		Capt PRIDAY from 240 to 3rd Section S.A.C. 2/Lt CRENTER to S.A.C. 2/Lt MATHIESON to D.A.C. OC G VARENNES	
	18		2/Lt MORRIS to 148 Th battery. Lt SPENSER & 148 Th battery, client persuade 10am. when (Capt.) BROWN.	
	19		Adj. to detach part of No 3 & No 4 Sections. 3 men killed & 3 wounded at Vue Th Battery	
	20		OC. + adjutant to funeral. BOUZINCOURT + dumps & camp much shelled 7pm	
	21		Col KERRIS on to leave. dump at conrie portally destroyed by shell fire. 3 men wounded, 1 bw killed + 3 wounded	
	22		OC calls E to m waiting arrangements for knew OC G VARENNES in afternoon.	
	23		2/Lt MICKELL to DAC on refiniment for Th battery. Remaining bw retrieved. B Cavallin 2/Lt HURNDALL reports from 240 Bde. Again finished.	
	24		Cross roads near dump shelled at 9.30 am a number of recalls cancelled owing to wet.	
	25		Church parade cancelled owing to wet. 49 rounds collected by DAC attached to 1st FORCEVILLE as ammunition	
	26		Adjutant sick. OC R.A.M.C. 48th Div. 47th 48th 49th Dw. OC inspects + inspection morning + noon evening 1 Sunday morning joined	
	27		OC. 249 Bw 85 H.B. & Am Supply. Given out 30 returned.	
	28		No 1 DAC section by Major from B Section detached with 144 inf Bde. Driver in No 2 Field wounded. OC R WARRENNES afternoon.	
	29		OC returned PRA section. also in field No 4 section at VARRENNES	
	30			
	31			

48th. DIVISION

48th. DIVISIONAL AMMUNITION COLUMN

SEPTEMBER 1916.

WAR DIARY or INTELLIGENCE SUMMARY

Army Form C. 2118.

HEADQUARTERS, 48th (S. M.) DIVISIONAL AMMUNITION COLUMN.
No. ......
Date: SEPT 1916

48/ D.A.C.

Place	Date	Hour	Summary of Events and Information	Remarks and references to Appendices
	Sept 1	1916	O.C. inspects 2 & 3 section in morning. V.O. inspects horses, 2000 rounds A drawn from 49" Dump	
	2		O.C. to S.A.A. position. No 3 section adjutant to WARRENNES	
	3		Church parade 10:30 am Chaplain BROWN. O.C. to inspect horses tat 4" section. 1500 rounds A drawn from 49" Dump	
	4		No Q.O. & No 2 section lines shelled 2:30 am, 4 "other ranks" wounded at Gun Depôt. Adjutant to WARRENNES	
	5		Brandell, S battery civilian moved. New drawn from 49" Gun dump	
	6		O.C. & 3/O Brigade at Q.O. in morning. O.C. & and section (Cpl WHITE to hospital)	
	7		Adjutant to BOUZINCOURT. O.C. to with dear stable	
	8		O.C. inspects 4 4 section. WARRENNES Corporal WHITE returns to duty	
	9		GOCRA judges drawing ammunition of position & 3/241 battery (two teams)	
	10		18 G.S. wagon lorries put into go-down from COLVILLERIS & VARRENNES. Vetchinen to gun position. Condition satisfied	
	11		Station J-BOUZINCOURT for Divisional Artillery	
	12		2/lt HURNDALL & 2n Corps. 2/lt RUSTINGTON to 241 Brigade. Lt P ... BELLE EGLISE, (1st to D.A.C.)	
	13		Staff Captain instructs moment of gun. Capt SPEAR to hospital. 2/lt TAYNTON to N.24 section, S/Spear & Bistaplety attached N.M.	
	14		O.C. No 2 section at midday. Capt DARLING appointed Y.O. to D.A.C.	
	15		240 & 243 Battles draw for station. Part 5 D.A.C. transmit in charge of Capt ANDERSON. Remainder New & BOUZINCOURT	
	16		O.C. relieves position D.A.C. ammunition. transmit from old Q.O. to new from 3 Ghan report	
	17		10 men train camp at AVELUT. 18 wagon tram. Infantry Brigade are east. 4 reinforce section New Officer attached wrote on	
	18		Congratulatory message in from Hr. M. the King - O.C. 2 Battalions - Capt WARRENNES Capt BROWN - Cpl VALLANCEY wounded.	
	19		No Q.O - remainders of 2 & 3 sections to ALBERT Gully. B.S.O.C. & W. GREENFIELD to 242 Brigade 4/Lt WYKIE killed - Cpt HANNAN killed near Hq run	
	20		4/Lt TIERMAN & GILLIGAN to 240 Brigade. 28 horses killed belonging to their units. O.C. - BOUZINCOURT to transmit up part of section	
	21		Dump near LA BOISELLE than 1/shell fully & two horses drawn down. T.M. ammunition received in part of section	
	22		COTRA men to dump started near dump for ammunition artillery	
	23		Capt ANDERSON learns O.C. Caution. O.C. ? 1 & 3 sections in morning 2410 2" units two famed by Brt	
	24		18 men to 3 rest camp at AVELUT 4/Lt Bulletin. O.C. 7 No 2 section complete to establish. S/Lt E.G. DAVIES reports from leave	
	25		Lt PIKE. Knapfield Gun position complete to establish. S/Lt E.G. DAVIES reports from leave	
	26		O.C. 4 section. 4/Lt COMBLES TAKEN O.C. 4 section	
	27		TUESDAY AVELUT COMBLES TAKEN O.C. K" section	
	28		Visits ETCOURT returns thirty on ambulance 4/Lt West killed Kindness in morning	
	29		4/Lt E. DAVIES posted K 241 Brigade 4/Lt West killed	
	30		O.C. & 2/Lt WEST's funeral at AVELUT. S/Officer report for duty from 63 Division 4/Lt HARMAN-HOUSTEN O.C. to referred to 4 section	
			L'S HUDSON and VAUX to No 3 Section. 2/Lts WHITEFORD & FILMER to No 3 section. 4/Lt HARMAN-HOUSTEN O.C. to BOUZINCOURT	

P.G. Arrender
Lieut

48th DIVL. AMMUNITION COLUMN.

WAR DIARY

OF

48th (South Mid.) DIVISIONAL AMMUNITION COLUMN. R.F.A.

FOR

NOVEMBER 1916.

Volume XXIV

HEADQUARTERS,
48th (S. M.) DIVISIONAL
AMMUNITION COLUMN.

No ....
Date... 3.12.16

Army Form C. 2118.

HEADQUARTERS,
46th (S.M.) DIVISIONAL
AMMUNITION COLUMN.
No ....
Date 3.12.16

VOLUME XXIV
NOVEMBER 1916

WAR DIARY
or
INTELLIGENCE SUMMARY
(Erase heading not required.)

Instructions regarding War Diaries and Intelligence Summaries are contained in F. S. Regs., Part II. and the Staff Manual respectively. Title Pages will be prepared in manuscript.

Place	Date	Hour	Summary of Events and Information	Remarks and references to Appendices
In the field	Nov 1st 1916		C.O. with ADC AMC etc AMB 4th Division Staff Capt. R.A. visited Mablethorpe. Lt. Pearse reported that approval commenced of 1st section. C.O. to 3rd section	
	Nov 2nd		List for 3rd section starting selected. C.O. to 3rd section	
	3		Staff Captain & C.C. commenced enquiries re men.	
	4		C.O. to B echelon. C.O. to 1st section	
	5		Church parade 9.30 am. in recreation room. Lt. Capt. Friday three cite for Hatting. C.O. to 2nd section	
	6		Major Spear to hospital for day. Estcourt, Charman, Whiteford & Perrins 17 hrs a.m. to 241 Bde.	
	7		C.O. to 240 Bde. HQ. about 3rd section Hatting. C.O. to other divisions	
	8		C.O. Staff Captain to Flish Army Saw Lieut Randolph R.E.	
	9		C.O. to B echelon & to Khalk Quarry with Lt. Randolph	
	10		Site allowed for 3rd section Hatting by A.A.Q.M.G. 3rd section moved to Quarry Hattings & locations etc. 3rd section huts & fuel moved	
	11		C.O. to B echelon. 5 subalterns returned from leave	
	12		Church parade 10 am. in recreation room. B.S.M. Gray attacked No.4 + B.S.M. Ridel No.8	
	13		Capt Anderson takes command of No.4 section	
	14		O.C. to No.3 Bty & Standings of Chinpas & Marlincourt to Maucharys	
	15		G.O.C.R.A. O.C. to B echelon. Lt. Pfar. R.E. on leave. Surplus B.S.M. + B.S.M.s. three	
	16		Boxing competition in recreation room. G.O.C.R.A. inspects horses. 2 H/nos & 1 Return	
			for duty. 3 Military Medals. L.Bdrs. inspected. L.A.A.R.S.	
	17		G.O.C.R.A. + O.C. BAC to B echelon & Louez Shemoer & Echelon, section Commanders Conference at 5.30	

WAR DIARY or INTELLIGENCE SUMMARY

Army Form C. 2118.

VOLUME XXIV
NOVEMBER 1916 (cont'd)

HEADQUARTERS,
48th (S.M.) DIVISIONAL AMMUNITION COLUMN.
Date 3.12.16

Place	Date	Hour	Summary of Events and Information	Remarks and references to Appendices
In the Field	Nov 18th 1916		O.C. 6/B echelon moved my own horses. Gr. Linegard wounded in cart - [illegible]	
	19		Ehrad horse 9.30am G.O.C. R.A. present.	
	20		Lt. K. Biddell. FLOWERS & NALL moves sent in on experimentary [illegible]. Gave up dealing with steam lorries ammunition on lorries.	
	21		O.C. inspected No. 8 Section mules, afterwards to B echelon to see my own horses No.1 section horses inspected 3.15	
	22		O.C. inspected No.3 section mules 9.45am, afterwards to No.4 section 2/Lt FLOWERS Maud Jun No. 8.A Lt MARSHALL to 26" D.A.	
	23		2/Lt FLOWERS to No. D.A. O.C inspected all B echelon animals, 51 reinforcements [illegible]	
	24		O.C & Staff Cpt. Thom to BARLEY to remove 6 immunes to [illegible]	
	25		O.C. to B echelon. 2/Lt VICKERS on leave V.O. JACKSON to the C.O.	
	26		GOCRA & Church Parade 9.30am. Received notice of the Meal of No 3 section conference 2/Lt Green RH, to move 2/Lt POTTER to 49 D.A. No 2 of Lt Duff Green DA & change to the 1 section times.	
	27		O.C. to B echelon to see my own horses [illegible] behind. Ammts landed over ETS (from 12 noon to NURNDA return from VII Corps. 2/Lt COLLINS from section	
	28		O.C. inspected No.4 section 10.30am 2/Lt PEARCE returned from leave	
	29		Left to BARLEY from with inoculating Staff O.C. No 4 section wrote to 46 D.A. re trains	
	30		O.C. to BARLEY. Adjutant with inoculating party to TAKNAS	

G.C. [signature]
Lieut.
ADJT.
48th DIVL. AMMUNITION COLUMN.

Vol XXI

WAR DIARY.

OF.

48th (South Midland) DIVISIONAL
AMMUNITION COLUMN. R.F.A.

FOR THE MONTH OF

DECEMBER 1916.

Volume ~~XXV~~

HEADQUARTERS,
48th (S. M.) DIVISIONAL
AMMUNITION COLUMN.

No ....
Date 1.1.16.

WAR DIARY
or
INTELLIGENCE SUMMARY

(Erase heading not required.)

Army Form C. 2118.

HEADQUARTERS,
48th (S.M.) DIVISIONAL
AMMUNITION COLUMN.

No. VOLUME 2.5
Date DECEMBER 1916

Instructions regarding War Diaries and Intelligence Summaries are contained in F. S. Regs., Part II. and the Staff Manual respectively. Title Pages will be prepared in manuscript.

Place	Date	Hour	Summary of Events and Information	Remarks and references to Appendices
In the field	Dec 1st/16		D.A.C. to TALMAS. LT ASSINDER with billeting party to FRECHENCOURT. Capts. COOPER & FORSYTH to D.A.C. from England.	
	2nd		D.A.C. to FRECHENCOURT. Section Commanders to conference at D.A.C. HQ. in evening.	
	3rd		Capt HEWITT arrives from ENGLAND	
		10 A.M.	O.C. No 4 Section & Adjt to new standing up for No 4 Sect near ALBERT. Horses in 4th Sect sent	
	4th		to 2nd & 3rd Section in exchange for mules —	
	5th		Capt COOPER in command of No 3 & Capt FORSYTH in command No 2 Section. Capt HEWITT & party of	
			2 Bom. & 9 men to A.R.P. 2 G.S. wagons from No 4 to HQ. 240 Bde at 7.30 A.M. 2 G.S. wagons complete	
			with Ammunition from No 4 to No 2 & 3 Sect ho	
			4th Sect to ALBERT. 2 Lt CONEY reports to D.A.C. O.C. to ALBERT in morning. Capts PRIDAY & SMITH-CARINGTON to ENGLAND.	
	6th		O.C. to B Echelon at ALBERT. Promotion of Sgt WEST to B.S.M. confirmed. 2 Lt CONEY to No 1 Sect ho	
	7th		T.M² Kent. FRECHENCOURT. Adjt - to B. ECHELON. O.C. inspects 1, 2 + 3 Section	
	8th		LT TAYNTON on leave. O.C. to WARLOY in morning. Capt GREEN appointed V.O. to A BERELON. O.C. inspects	
	9th		Sub annuals into V.O.	
	10th		CHURCH PARADE. 10 A.M. O.C. & Adjt to 4 Sect at ALBERT. LT JUCKES from leave.	
	11th		LT CONEY to No 4 Sect. O.C. inspects horses of 2 +3 Section. Meeting of O.C. Sections representatives from	
			each Section re Canteen.	
	12th		Adjt to WARLOY. O.C. inspects 1, 2 + 3 Section. O.C. & Adjt to AMIENS. 3 rom Nations issued	
	13th		in morning. Adjt to ALBERT meeting in football at Div H. Qrs. Free man shewing	
	14th		O.C. inspects 1st Round Section in morning. LT PALMER A. attached to No 2 Sect. Town Major over re standings	
			in lieu parade by No 2 Sect ho	
	15th		O.C. & 4 Sect at ALBERT. LT LINES returns from leave. Adjt to 4th Sect ALBERT 1st two mules moved to T.H.B. 10 G.S wagons & 12 mule Bdr	
	16th		O.C. to B Echelon at ALBERT. Walk morphe moved.	
	17th		G.O.C. R.A. inspects horses to [illegible] Riding school & [illegible] & mules to A. Echelon	
	18th		& expresses his entire satisfaction.	

Army Form C. 2118.

WAR DIARY
or
INTELLIGENCE SUMMARY.
(Erase heading not required.)

Instructions regarding War Diaries and Intelligence Summaries are contained in F.S. Regs., Part II. and the Staff Manual respectively. Title pages will be prepared in manuscript.

Place	Date	Hour	Summary of Events and Information	Remarks and references to Appendices
In the field.	19/Dec/16		Reinf of 10 came with personnel, 10 Gunners, 3 NCO's & Lt GILLIGAN from 4 Sect by No 1 Sect. including Lt BLOOR.	
	20 Dec		OC inspects No 1, 2 & 3 Sections in morning. Officers ride in afternoon. OC sees Sect'n Commdrs. receipt.	
	21		Reinf of 10 came with personnel 6 gunners, 3 new Lt COLLINS by No 5, 2 & 3 including Lt PALMER. V.O. inspects all horses. 17 evacuated to Base, aged. OC 6 B Echelon — details OC inspects all sections of A Echelon. Adjt Lt 4th Sect tRA.	
	22		OC A Section in morning. 60 men to bomb school for instruction. 2 H.D. horses from No 24	
	23		relieved by 2 from No 1 Sect.	
	24		Church Parade 10 AM. Chaplain B. on own. GOCRA & Staff Capt's own in afternoon.	
	25		Xmas Day.	
	26		Sgt Bennett BSM to No 1 on for station. 10 came from A Echelon relieve 10 came from No 2 (2 No 1, 3 No 2, 5 No 3) 50 men to MIDDLE WOOD — BX Ammunition from A Echelon to X 15 central dump. Lt GILLIGAN to No 4.	
	27		OC Lt B 2 dealer at ALBERT. Lt GUNYON on leave No 11BX to PEAKE WOOD	
	28		Lt COLLINS to BAZENTIN dump with 12 new AX of No 3 Sect's to PEAKE WOOD Adjt to CONTAY re defective AX & BX (F10) A ammunition (wagons) (4 No 1 + 5 No 2) 6 x 15 Cwt lorries	
	29		— At ammunition (9 wagons No 2 Sect) to PEAKE WOOD dump. OC 6 AMIENS re Gun dump.	
	30		Lt MOTTRAM reported as Adjt. Lt ASSINDER to 241 B.L.R.F.A. CAPT BURBIDGE reports to from B Corps AMM.PARK.	
	31		Horse AnSub. Section Commanders conference —	

E. Mottram Lt.
ADJT.
48th DVL. AMMUNITION COLUMN.

WAR DIARY

OF

48th (S.M.) DIVISIONAL AMMUNITION COLUMN. R.F.A.

FOR

JANUARY. 1917.

Volume. XXV.

WAR DIARY or INTELLIGENCE SUMMARY

Army Form C. 2118.

January 1917 Volume XXV

Place	Date	Hour	Summary of Events and Information	Remarks and references to Appendices
In the field	Jan 1st		Brigade Major at HQ re reorganisation of D.A.C. - C.O. to B Echelon & thought back Capt. ANDERSON. A.A.P.M.G. called re SOUP KITCHEN at FRENCHENCOURT. SOUP KITCHEN established and in full swing.	
	2nd		Teams sent to relieve B Echelon teams. Lt HALL relieves Lt BLOOR at B Echelon. CO awarded D.S.O. & S.M. BROOM, D.C.M. (LONDON GAZETTE 31 Dec. 16)	
	3rd		Wood cutting working parties. Commenced cording up Road at water trough - CO on leave and Capt. ANDERSON took over command - Lt TAYNTON to hospital. Capt. FARRELL attached as V.O. When O i/c to MIDDLE WOOD to replace casualties.	
	4th		Capt. Adjt. to B Echelon. ALBERT, PEAKE WOOD DUMP, BAZENTIN DUMP & LA BOISSELLE. "A" Echelon interchanged teams & personnel so that each Section had its own teams & personnel. A.S. Wagon sent to 242 Bde R.F.A. 40 reinforcements arrive FRENCHENCOURT. 20 men relieved at MIDDLE WOOD.	
	5th		Baths. No clean clothing. No 1 & No 4 Sections interchanged so that each Section got its own (teams & personnel). Lt LINES to B Echelon & Lt HALL to No 3 Sect.	
	6th		No 3 & No 4 interchange (teams & personnel) so that each Section had their own. 20 men relieved at MIDDLE WOOD. 2nd Lt (Temp Capt) FORSYTH invalided to 2nd LF on attachment in pt Lieut (d. 1 Dec. 16). Lt HURNDALL with 4/4 mule teams sent to HQ Q23 46 Div Train to await 144 Inf. Bde. Capt BURBIDE & M.O. (Capt SMITH) proceed on leave. Capt. D. DAVIDSON, 240 Bde R.F.A. acts as M.O. 30 reinforcements sent to B Echelon - 6 reinforcements to 240 Bde R.F.A.	
	7th		Church Parade followed by celebration. Capt. ANDERSON G.R.A H Qrs - Fellowreinforcements arrived. Capt. S.C. WILSON, Lt P.D. FISHER, Lt E.C. BATCHELOR & Lt A.S. BLYTHE attached respective to No 2, No 2, No 3 & No 1 Sections. A.D.V.S. at FRECHENCOURT.	
	8th		2/CRA (Lt Col. LORD WYNFORD) & Bde Major at D.A.C. MAJOR J.A. WEDDERBURN OGILVY 2nd SCOTTISH HORSE reported D.A.C. for attachment. Defective Ammunition 179 A.X. & 70 B.X. returned to Railhead. Lt F. FLETCHER reported from 17th D.A.	
	9th		2/CO. Maj. OGILVY A.D.J.T. went round Sections. A.M.T.O. unable to lend 20 a car to visit ARPs 2/CO visits No 1 & 2 Section Side lines with V.O. MIDDLE WOOD relief - A.D.J.T at early stables - 2/CO no peruta watering parades -	
	10th		10 reinforcements arrived - MIDDLE WOOD relief	

Army Form C. 2118.

WAR DIARY
or
INTELLIGENCE SUMMARY

(Erase heading not required.)

Place	Date	Hour	Summary of Events and Information	Remarks and references to Appendices
In the field	Jany 11th		4 C.O. inspected A Echelon harness & fattening lines – Lt TAYNTON member of F.G.C.M.	
	" 12		All gun books though return to H.Q. & stores from A Echelon. New pump installed at Wate Trough on A.S. wagon that to 1st Div Brit School & to R.A. Canteen 242 Bde.	
	" 13		4 C.O. & MAJOR OGILVY to B Echelon. Adjt to Field Cashier. MIDDLEWOOD returned. Sick Bay empty. M.O. on leave. Capt MURRAY R.A.M.C. 242 Bde acts as M.O.	
	" 14		No church parade. Bde Major & Staff Capt to see 4 C.O. re reorganisation – B Echelon relieved 87 Howers wds the wagons	
	" 15		B Echelon details sent to join No 3 Sect. B.S.M. GRAY reported. Lt FISHER to hospital. Lt HORNDALL to B Echelon.	
	" 16		Telephone installed. Capt FARRELL A.V.C. to Div HdQrs. MAJOR OGILVY to 242 Bde. Chaplain BROWN (C.F.) to D.A.C. Trench Mortar Batteries arrived & billeted in FRECHENCOURT. No 2782 Gnr BILLINGTON remanded by 4 C.O. for F.G.C.M.	
	" 17		Lt PALMER returned from B Echelon to 2nd Sect. B.S.M. Sheldon to Base. C.O. returned from leave. C.O. & Capt ANDERSON round No 1 & 3 Sections. V.O. & Adjt round sick lines. 2 N.C.O's to relief at MIDDLE WOOD.	
	" 18		Lt PALMER to BAZENTIN A.R.P. to relieve Lt COLLINS.	
	" 19		C.O. inspected A Echelon in marching order & afterwards held a conference of officers & B.S.M. of Sections 1 & 2. Capt ANDERSON returned to B Echelon. Lt COLLINS reported 3rd Section M.O. inspected Sick Lines. Capt GAUNT A.V.C. returned from leave – 17 men for remounts arrived BAZENTIN dump handed over to 1st D.A.	
			Lt PALMER returned to No 2 Sect. Reorganisation completed & 3rd Sect. became 242 Bde Amn Col	
	" 20		C.O. inspected the men of No's 1 & 2 Sections – 12 men to MIDDLE WOOD relief. C.O. inspected wagon parks.	
	" 21			
	22		No 2 Sect's re-inspected by Adjt (the C.O. Great improvement. No 142961 Dr PYATT. A. received supposed self inflicted injury to 45 Div School in afternoon. Capt COOPER sent on billeting officer to FOULLOY.	

Army Form C. 2118.

WAR DIARY
or
INTELLIGENCE SUMMARY.
(Erase heading not required.)

Instructions regarding War Diaries and Intelligence Summaries are contained in F.S. Regs., Part II. and the Staff Manual respectively. Title pages will be prepared in manuscript.

Place	Date	Hour	Summary of Events and Information	Remarks and references to Appendices
In the field	Jan. 1923		Interpreter GENTIS to FOULLOY to assist Capt COOPER. All S.A.A., P.W.A. & grenades returned to Railhead CONTAY. C.O. inspected wagon/parks. MIDDLE WOOD working Parks returned.	
	24		Cart to BEHENCOURT for Gnr. BILLINGTON's F.G.C.M. 152 Remounts arrived FRECHENCOURT & distributed to Brigades + R.E.s 57 reinforcements arrived. PEAKE WOOD dump relieved.	
	25		Asst + R.S.M to HAMELET to Billet. 6 p.m. Sect. Comndrs. Conference re orders re moving. Warm G.S. Cart to Batteries + T.M.s	
	26		A Echelon left FRECHENCOURT at 7.45 A.M. marched to HAMELET via BEHENCOURT, PONT NOYELLES, DAOURS, AUBIGNY & FOULLOY. B Echelon from ALBERT to AUBIGNY. Staff Capt. Bde Maj. R.A. + HAMELET. Lt. F.W. EURIDGE reported from 255 Bde R.F.A., 1st Div. + attached to No. 1 Sectn. team postponed.	
	27		Staff Capt. at HAMELET. C.O. + Adjt. to B Schelon at AUBIGNY. Genl. WARD visited A Schelon lines. C.O. inspected Services under C.O. Capt. BURBIDGE to CAPPY re Billeting.	
	28		T.M.s	
	29		Lt. EURIDGE to 4th Army Anti-Gas School PONT NOYELLES. Capt. BURBIDGE + Interpreter GENTIS to CAPPY re Billeting. C.O. inspected A Schelon Horses.	
	30		C.O. + Adjt. to R.A.H.Q. C.O. inspected B Schelon Horses. Lt. HALL reported from 4th Army T.M. School.	
	31		Gnr. BILLINGTON's sentence of 56 days F.P. No. 1 promulgated. C.O. + Adjt. to R.A.H.Q. C.O. + Staff Capt. to position of new A.R.P.	

1577 Wt. W10791/1773 500,000 1/15 D.D. & L. A.D.S.S./Forms/C. 2118.

WK 23

WAR DIARY
OF
48th (South Midland) DIVISIONAL AMMUNITION COLUMN. R.F.A.
FOR THE MONTH OF
FEBRUARY — 1917

Volume XXVII

HEADQUARTERS,
48th (S. M.) DIVISIONAL
AMMUNITION COLUMN.

No ....
Date... 1.3.17

Army Form C. 2118.

HEADQUARTERS,
45th (2. M.) DIVISIONAL
AMMUNITION COLUMN.
No. Vol.Jm. XXVII
Date. FEBRUARY.

WAR DIARY
or
INTELLIGENCE SUMMARY.
(Erase heading not required.)

Instructions regarding War Diaries and Intelligence Summaries are contained in F.S. Regs., Part II. and the Staff Manual respectively. Title pages will be prepared in manuscript.

Place	Date 1917	Hour	Summary of Events and Information	Remarks and references to Appendices
In the field	1st Feb.		Lt. JUCKES + 25 men to B7. ARP. Lt. PALMER + 12 men to CAPPY. R.S.M. to CAPPY.	
	2nd		Hd.Qrs. wk. Adjt. preceded DAC to CAPPY. Lt. CONEY from leave. Adjt. to Stoke, walk through disinfected & stables cleaned. Adjt. wk. S.C.R.A. to West-B.Sch. Soltems	
	3rd		arrived CAPPY 2pm. Issue of ammunition from OLIMPE dump to full baking wagons. Adjt. to Ammunition dump.	
	4th		Lt. PALMER finished issuing ammunition from OLIMPE dump. C.O. inspected dumps Adjt. to B.Sch. Horse shows. No. 39617 Dr. STOVOLD remanded by C.O. for F.G.C.M.	
	5th		Lt. EURIDGE returned from Anti gas course. Capt. COOPER returned to duty to command 4 No 2 Sec 2. C.O. & ARP. Adjt. to RAHQ & Gaw. Capt. A/DAH for Amm.ln Supply.	
	6th		C.O. + Adjt. to RAHQ. Adjt. to ARP. HQ.A.C. hoar to arrange FRENCH relief. S.C.R.A. + ARP. Capt. Comm. dr. at ARP. Lt. PALMER pdd to T.M.B.	
	7th		1,000,000 SAA arrived & distributed to A.Sch. Adjt. to RAHQ. C.O. + Adjt. issue DA.DOS. + to ARP.	
	8th		Lt. CONEY to ARP. 4 the 4/c 4 R.E. Station. 2 Candidates for commissions to ENGLAND. C.O. + Adjt. to B.Sch. ARP. 300,000 SAA issued for B.Sch. Lt.GILLIGAN pdd. to B/340. Telephone installed. Gas lecture by Lt. EURIDGE.	
	9th		C.O. to B.Sch. S.C.R.A. at DAC. Lt. BLOOR returned from leave.	
	10th		leave stopped. C.O. inspected 1st Sec 3. C.O. to ARP. Lt. HURNDALL & M.G.R.A. 4th Army. No. 81547 Dr. McKINLEY remanded by C.O. for F.G.C.M. C.O. to ARP. at T.M. Ammunition.	
	11th		C.O. to HQ.R.A. at T.M. Amm. C.O. + Adjt. to B.Sch. + inspected No 2 Sec 2. Lt. EURIDGE enlivered Lt. JUCKES at ARP. T.M. Ammn. in forward dump. Adjt. & ARP. Q. RICHARDSON remanded for F.G.C.M. Lt. FORSYTH returned from 45 Div. Sch. at Rocal Strain control commenced.	
	12th		C.O. to ARP. Lt. FULLERTON returned from leave.	
	13th		F.G.C.M. Dr. STOVOLD. B.Sch. moved into CANAL CAMP. 6 Officers + 130 O.R. re-inforcements arrived. Lt. BONHAM EDWARDS to 241 Bde. Lt. PLOWMAN + HAMILTON to 151 Sec 2. Lt. BYRNE to K 2nd Sec 2. Lt. LESLIE to 4 Sec 2. Lt. FISHER returned 2nd Sec 2 from leave. C.O. to ARP. Lt. EURIDGE awarded CROIX de GUERRE.	
	14th		SCS warm. Ent. E. 14/3 Inf. Bde. 270. 270 SAA + 2000 No 5 grenades to 145 H/Bde. Adjt. to CORBIE to stat. 45 Div. Aut. Mens. Fund. Lt. T.K. HALL pdd. to V. U15 T.M.B.	
	15th		C.O. to ARP. DADMS inspected camp. Welcolfined. STS warm. Ent. to 145 Inf. Bde.	

3.GS warm ent. to 145 T.M.

WAR DIARY or INTELLIGENCE SUMMARY

Army Form C. 2118.

HEADQUARTERS,
48th (S. M.) DIVISIONAL
AMMUNITION COLUMN
Volume XXVII
FEB 1917

Place	Date 1917	Hour	Summary of Events and Information	Remarks and references to Appendices
In the field	Feb. 16		Lt. BUSTARD reported Adjt. to ARP & 2nd BAC. S&S & AX & Aml (Bde) at 7pm to draw on ration. Reinforcements to 1st Bde as follows 37 OR to 240, 43 to 241.	
	17		2400 AX, 1000 A & 2501 BX drawn from railhead. Adjt. to railhead & ARP. CO to ARP working parties sent to Bde as follows 15 NCO & men to 240 Bde, Lt HAMILTON + 35 men to 241st Bde. Thos Precautions before Ch. Parade Q. 9AM Harness competition won by 2nd Sect.	
	18		Lt. PLOWMAN to BOIS OLYMPE as Camp Commandant.	
	19		FGCM at HQ DAC tried Lt RICHARDSON, CPL McKINLEY & Pte PYATT. 500, 2" T.M., 1000 AX collected from MERIGNOLLES railhead. #65 waggons to draw RE balks. S&S waggons to D.T.M.O.	
	20		5000 A & 1000 BX drawn from MERIGNOLLES. 13.0 rounds 9.45" T.M. Amn delivered to ARP by road. S&S waggons for D.T.M.O. CO & Adjt to ARP. Conduct of talk commenced at rest.	
	21		Adjt to RAT HQ & ARP. French Grenades collected & returned to railhead. 4000 A, 2000 AX, 1000 BX 100. 2" T.M. & 552 D Grenades & Very lights & cartridges collected from MERIGNOLLES. S&S waggons for D.T.M.O.	
	22		2000 A, 2000 AX, 2000 BX drawn from railhead, also Very lights & cartridges. S&S waggons RE's, S&S for D.T.M.O. & S&S for T.M. 30 mile wire, 4 miles cart for use by D.D.R.	
	23		3000 A, 1000 AX, 1000 BX, 30 rds 9.45" T.M. drawn from railhead. S&S & 160 Tumbrils by S&S. 1st duck boards, 3 S&S, D.T.M.O. 2 S&S, 143 Inf Bde. Lt. FULLERTON to 240 Bde.	
	24		2000 A, 800 BX drawn from railhead. 26 S&S for duck boards, 3 S&S D.T.M.O. Drew 300 Pt Prot. for conducting to ARP. S&S for RE & w timber for OPs. Maj. TODD D.S.O. relieved 15 officers on "GUNNERY".	
	25		2 G.S. for D.T.M.O. 8 S&S for timber for OPs. Ch. Parade Q. 9.30 AM. D.A.A. + Q.M.G. for CAMP. Lt. FORSYTH to anti gas School. S&S to RE's at CAPPY. G.G.S. for iron girders. S&S for timber for Ops. Drew Gun Cotton to replace expenditure. Lt EURIDGE instructed on use of Bar Respirator Balls.	
	26		4 G.S. at 9 AM to RE's S&S in timber for OPS	
	27		12 G.S. to RE's CAPPY. 6 G.S. waggons for timber for OPs. 4 G.S. for D.T.M.O. 3 G.S. for D.T.M.O. 1 G.S. for CAMP COMMANDANT. 1396 AX drawn from railhead	

F. Moltzan Lt Adjt
45 DAC

1577 Wt.W10791/1773 500,000 1/15 D.D.&L. A.D.S.S./Forms/C. 2118.

War Diary March 1917,

48 Divisional Ammunition Column.

WAR DIARY or INTELLIGENCE SUMMARY

Army Form C. 2118.

Place	Date	Hour	Summary of Events and Information	Remarks and references to Appendices
In the field	1917 1st Mar.		17 G.S. wagons working parties. 4 limb. Amm. wagons lent to A/241. C.O. & Adjt to ARP. 4 G.S. lent to D.T.M.O. 3 reinforcements to T.M's	
	2nd "		19 G.S. wagons on working parties. Lts FISHER & BYRNE on course at 4 Army Art'y Sch. Centre & Area stores returned to D.A.D.O.S. Adjt to ARP.	
	3rd "		Drew 2500 rounds 18 pdr from railhead. C.O. & Adjt to ARP. 24 G.S. wagons on working parties	
	4th "		16 G.S. wagons on working parties. Ch. parade 9.30 A.M. C.O. to RA HQ & Adjt to ARP. Lt CRANE posted to D/241	
	5th "		21 G.S. wagons on working parties. 12 teams lent to A/26 1st Div. for withdrawal of battery from action.	
	6th "		Lt FORSYTH returned from 4 Army Art'y Gas School. Lt EURIDGE attached to B/240.	
	7th "		23 G.S. wagons on working parties. C.O. & Sect'y Commdr reconnoitred forward position for wagon lines. 6td gunners arrived from batteries (in exchange with 48 A.S.P. 48 fifteen reinforcements arrived attached as follows Lt RONDON to 10th Lt ALLDAY to No 2. Lt ISAAC & BOURNE to BSch. C.O. to RAHQ.	
	8th "		12 G.S. wagons on working parties.	
	9th "		17 G.S. wagons on working parties. Adjt to ARP. A.D.V.S. to see C.O. Gunners exchanged with 48 A.S.P.	
	10th "		16 G.S. wagons on working parties	
	11th "		C.O. to HQ RA. 12 G.S. wagons on working parties. Lt GUNYON returned from 48 Div Sch. Ch. Parade 9.15 A.M. Lt GRUNDY, MERRYWEATHER & BISHOP reported att. respectively to 10th, 2nd Sect. & B Sch. Lt GAMLIN reported from R.A. for instruction. C.D. & Adjt to ARP. A.D.V.S. inspected all animals. SCR & visited No 1 Sect Lines.	
	12th "		C.R.A. hoped to see D.A.C. reinforced pleasure at general condition of the units. also at the work that had been done. — 22 G.S. wagons on working parties.	
	13th "		24 G.S. wagons on working parties. (Lt TAYNTON, Lts ISAAC) BOURNE & BLOOR to (C/240) A/240 & B/240 respectively. Lt FORSYTH, BLYTHE, & ALLDAY to A/241, D/241 & C/241 respectively. Lt TUCKER to 48 Div Sch. Lt ISAAC returned from hosp. re. rank. to join Yeo.	
	14th " 15th "		16 G.S. wagons on working parties. Rifle drills for all ranks.	
	16th "		21 G.S. wagons on working parties. Capt. COOPER att'd RAHQ. Lt MOTTRAM to command 2nd Sect. Lt GUNYON posted to No 2 Sect & Lt FLETCHER to No 1 Sect. GO to conference at Div HQ at 3.30 p.m. Reports of division worked by Centre Commdrs DAC provided 50 three men representing 48 Div AMQ completed by CRA. in turn out. 17 G.S. wagons on working parties	
	17th "		C.O. to RAHQ. DAC moved Div. Bomb Dump. New walk trough completed issued at CANAL CAMP, CAPPY	

WAR DIARY or INTELLIGENCE SUMMARY

Army Form C. 2118.

Place	Date	Hour	Summary of Events and Information	Remarks and references to Appendices
In the field	17 March		1 G.S. Wagon smashed including artillery. New one obtained. Heavy left to B/240	
	18 "	9.30 AM	Ch. Parade. C.O. inspected all sections. A Sch. collected ammunition from battery positions & returned it to RPN.	
	19 "		A Sch. collected ammunition from battery positions & returned it to RPN.	
	20 "		143 & 1445 Inf Bde each returned 1 G.S. wagon to BSch.	
	21 "		24 G.S. wagons on working parties. CAPT PEARCE & Lt. GRUNDY, 71 O.R. took forward section to join Genl. WARDS FLYING COLUMN marching via HALLE to PERONNE. Lt. MOTTRAM returned from O.C. No.2 Sect. & was relieved by Capt. BURBIDGE. Lt. BISHOP appointed to command position of No.2 Sect. remaining at CANAL CAMP. C.O. to advanced section at PERONNE.	
	22 "		Adjt & R.S.M visited old battery positions & counted ammunition & then visited advanced section at PERONNE. 18 G.S wagons on working parties. Capt. BURBIDGE handed over to Lt. HAMILTON the Town Majorship of CANAL CAMP.	
	23 "		C.O. to advanced section at PERONNE. 16 G.S. wagons on working parties.	
	24 "		Lts COTTAM, CHAVASSE, BRADY, CARTER & 19 O.R reinforcements arrived. 10 L.D. Sect to 240 Bde.	
	25 "		Lts BYRNE & FISHER returned from 4th Army Art. Sch. Col. COLVILLE & B-M. R.A. to see C.O. A Sch & HQ moved to PERONNE. ASch filled with ammn. at RPN.	
	26 "		Re-establishment of forward ARP. A Sch. dumped all Spdr. & 4.5" ammn. proceeded to RPN, filled up, C.O. & Adjt reconnoitred journey ARP. C.O. & Col. COLVILLE decided on 1.2.D.5.4 as position for ARP. The 1st Sec. his Sect ammunition to ARP will very bad charges. B Sch sent 16 G.S. wagons on working parties drew A&B Sch rations, filled up with ammunition at RPN, emptied at new ARP & moved to ST RADEGONDE	
	27 "		Untraced ammunition recatalogued ammunition removed from RPN to ARP. S.C.R.A & D.B.O to see C.O. D.A.C. to take over all S.A.A. grenades, very lights &c.	
	28 "		Adjt to RPN to supervise removal of ammunition returns to Regt ARP. All 18 pdr. ammn moved.	
	29 "		Removal of Bx to ARP continued. C.O. to COURCELLES to reconnoitre wagon line for 1st Sect. Adjt to ARP. DBO called about the grenade dump.	
	30 "		C.O. & Adjt to ARP & BSch. C.O. & R.S.M to COURCELLES. No.1 Sect moved to COURCELLES Removal of Bx from RPN to ARP continued. 20 reinforcements arrived. C.O. to RAHO.	
	31 "		No.2 Sect & H.Qrs moved to COURCELLES. Adt reconnoitred A.R.Ps in vicinity of LONGAVESNES & TINCOURT. C.O. to BSch.	

F. Mottram Lt. Adjt
48 D.A.C.

WAR DIARY.
OF
48th (S.M.) DIVISIONAL AMMUNITION COLUMN. R.F.A.

FOR MONTH OF

APRIL 1917.

VOLUME XXIX

Army Form C. 2118.

WAR DIARY
or
INTELLIGENCE SUMMARY.

(Erase heading not required.)

Instructions regarding War Diaries and Intelligence Summaries are contained in F. S. Regs., Part II. and the Staff Manual respectively. Title pages will be prepared in manuscript.

HEADQUARTERS,
48th (S. M.) DIVISIONAL AMMUNITION COLUMN.

No. VOLUME XXIX
Date 30.4.17.

Place	Date	Hour	Summary of Events and Information	Remarks and references to Appendices
COURCELLES TINCOURT	APRIL 1st		Adjt to B.Sch & ARP at PERONNE & TINCOURT. New ARP to reconnoitre wagon lines. Continued moving ARP from PERONNE to COURCELLES.	
	2nd		HHQ2 & Echelon moved to TINCOURT. New ARP established at HAMEL & ammunition moved to there from COURCELLES. C.O. to Divl Grenade dump at PERONNE. Lt. GRUNDY in charge of HAMEL ARP. B Echelon moved from STE RADEGONDE to COURCELLES. III Corps Amm. Park commenced to make dump beside ARP.	
	3rd		Gun ammunition, grenades, S.A.A. to moved from PERONNE & COURCELLES to HAMEL.	
	4th		Removal of dumps at PERONNE & COURCELLES to HAMEL continued. C.O. to B.Sch. 2/Lts BRADY, CARTER, PLOWMAN, HAMILTON, BYRNE, COTTAM & CHAVASSE posted to Battery. 2/Lt HOBSON arrived from ENGLAND and a/c'd B Schelon.	
	5th		B.Sch. continued moving PERONNE & COURCELLES ARPS to HAMEL. C.O. to B.Sch. C.O. & Adjt reconnoitred battery positions & lines round of No 1 & 2 Sections.	
	6th		C.O. to B.Sch. Removal of PERONNE & COURCELLES ARPS completed. 300 rounds 18 pdr. salved from FLAUCOURT. C.O. reconnoitred battery positions.	
	7th		C.O. & Adjt to B.Sch. Rations drawn for horses to be attached from the Div. 11 G.S. wagons for can. lines arrived for the Div.	
	8th		EASTER DAY. C.O. round all see. Two ts selected of this horses for H.Q. battery q. line. 2/Lts SELLERS & CULVERWELL joined & attached to No. 1 & 2 Sec'ns respectively. Following arrived from 42 D.A.C. for attachment. 2 Officers 83 O.R., 50 mules & 104 H.D.	
	9th		Working party under R.S.M. prepared grenade dump near VILLERS FAUCON. 1 S.O.R. reinforcements arrived including Dr CRESSWELL charged with desertion. B.Sch. collected grenades from FLAUCOURT. C.O. & Adjt round A.Sch. lines. C.O. reconnoitred battery positions. Bde. Major & S.C.R.A. to see C.O. C.O. allotted 42 D.A.C. details to No 1 Sec'n for discipline. B.Sch. collected grenades & stores mostly from BIRCHES salvage dump.	
	10th		Adjt to start grenade dump at VILLERS FAUCON. B.Sch. move up grenades S.A.A. to from HAMEL. C.O. to new grenade dump Map Ref. E29 B.17. (Sheet 62C)	
	11th			
	12th		Adjt & R.S.M. reconnoitred wagon lines of STE. EMILIE. 1st Sec'n & 42 D.A.C. details moved to Railway cutting at E23 d 2.3. (Sheet 62C) in STE. EMILIE. 2nd Sec'n lent 6 G.S. to 5th Rifl. Suffolk Regt. C.O. & S.C.R.A. visited 1st Sec'n. C.O. & Adjt round 2nd Sec'n. B.Sch. continued moving grenade dump to VILLERS FAUCON.	
	13th		C.O. to B.Sch. S.C.R.A. called. Indents for ammunition in III Corps Amm. Park notified to Abbey to Corps. B.Sch. continued to move grenade dump.	
	14th		Adjt to No 1 Sec'n at STE EMILIE. B.Sch. continued to move grenade dump. No 2 Sec'n supplies No 1 Sec'n with ammunition.	
	15th		Adjt to No 1 Sec'n. D.B.D. called to see Adjt re shortage /of lbs delimator not enough left at SALVAGE DUMP for one more tank Stokes shells. 22. O.R. reinforcements & Lt. BATCHELOR from Base hospital at B.Sch.	

Army Form C. 2118.

WAR DIARY
or
INTELLIGENCE SUMMARY

(Erase heading not required.)

Instructions regarding War Diaries and Intelligence Summaries are contained in F.S. Regs., Part II. and the Staff Manual respectively. Title pages will be prepared in manuscript.

HEADQUARTERS,
48th (S.M.) DIVISIONAL
AMMUNITION COLUMN.
No. 30.4.17
VOLUME XXIX

Place	Date	Hour	Summary of Events and Information	Remarks and references to Appendices
TINCOURT	April 16th (Cont'd)	17:15	Sergt. Inst. to 240 Bde to look after Bde tn. horses. Capt ANDERSON & 2.O.R. on leave. Lt CONEY & ARP move to VILLERS FAUCON. Lt COPER & ARP move to VILLERS FAUCON. C.O. & SCRA reconnoitred new ARP. C.O. round No 2 Sect. Adj't (see SCRA.	
VILLERS-FAUCON	16th		HQ move to E29.a.6.0 Sheet 62cw VILLERS FAUCON. 20 o.R. reinforcements arrived. Sergt. Inst. to 241 Bde. for fatigue line.	
		19:30	Adj't proceed with to FGCM. ARP very busy. Capt COOPER member of FGCM. No 2 Sect ? build Amn. Issue sent up to VILLERS FAUCON to assist in Ammunition Supply.	
	20th		C.O. to see No 2 Sect at TINCOURT. C.O. & Capt COOPER reconnoitred wagon line for No 3 Sect at VILLERS FAUCON. D.A.C. takes over water trough at STE EMILIE. 16 reinforcements to 241 Bde., 9 to 240 Bde.	
	21st		B Sch move from COURCELLES to TINCOURT, & No 2 Sect from TINCOURT to VILLERS FAUCON area. C.O. to see move. SCRA to see C.O. 42 DivnA.C. details return to HQ DAC. HQ's complimented by Genl BUDWORTH, MGRA 4th Army.	
	22nd		Wati syphoned from STE EMILIE reservoir to Rly cutting to avoid observation from enemy balloons. C.O. inspected 2 No 1 lines Genl WARD passed through No 1 Sect lines. Barbed wire drawn from TINCOURT to wire in & round foilers. Lt CULVERWELL admitted hospital.	
	23rd		Capt BURBIDGE & Lt HOBSON with 25 drivers per wagon & 16 per section collected H.O.L.D. & 57 mules from GUILLAUCOURT. Adj't & SCRA at TINCOURT. Adj't to B Sch - SCRA to DAC.	
	24th		Adj't & RSM to see remounts in morning. Adj't & SCRA to see remounts in afternoon. C.O. to see Batt'y of QUILLEMONT FME. 6094 rounds delivered by DAC to Batteries night of 24/25.	
	25th		B Sch emptied ARP from TINCOURT. C.O. to B Sch. Genl WARD inspected Amn on its to be distributed 25 cars from HQ 42. Inst. to move Cavalry. Teams comp handed by Genl WARD. 2. O.R. on leave.	
	26th		C.O. to B Sch. to distribute new amn mules. 14 surplus to establishment. Adj't to No 2 Sect & ARP. C.O. & Adj't round No 2 Sect & ARP.	
	27th		C.O. & Adj't reconnoitred mns n apn line for B Sch at MARQUAIX, & then went to RAHO. Adj't & ARP 272 rounds 4 defective ammunition (NCT (4)) found in Amn ? from Lt Corp Amn Park.	
	28th		B Sch moved from BOUCLY to MARQUAIX. C.O. & Adj't to B Sch. No 3 Sect & ARP.	
	29th		C.O. & Adj't to RAHO. Received No 1 & 2 Sect's & ARP. Sect Commdrs conference 2.30pm - Lt LINES to see C.O. Church parade 6.30pm. Capt ANDERSON returned from leave.	
	30th		C.O. to B Sch. SCRA 48 Div & SCRA 4th Div. called with reference to relief of 48 DAC by 42 DAC.	

F. McRae Lt Adj't
48 DAC

Vol 26

War Diary

of

48th (S.M) Divisional Ammunition Column. R.F.A.

for

May - 1917.

Volume XXX.

WAR DIARY or INTELLIGENCE SUMMARY

Army Form C. 2118.

Vol XXX
MAY 1917

Place	Date 1917	Hour	Summary of Events and Information	Remarks and references to Appendices
VILLERS-FAUCON	1st MAY		S.C.R.A. 4th Div. Adjt. F.Sect's Commdr. 42 D.A.C. to see C.O. re relief. Officer & staff from 42 D.A.C. attd. to A.R.P. for instruction before taking over. All Amm. on A.R.P. counted.	
BUIRE	2nd "		46 D.A.C. moved to BUIRE. Half gun section of 1st Sect'n remained with complement of ammunition at STE EMILIE, attached to 42 D.A.C. Half gun section of 2nd Sect'n sent to BOUCLY in TINCOURT & attached 59 D.A.C. A.R.P. & Grenade S.A.A.etc. dump handed over to 42 D.A.C. Adjt. to detailed portion of 2 Sect's at BOUCLY. C.O. 45/R.A.H.Q.	
	3rd "		Adjt. C.O. & Adjt. of No 2 Sect early visits. 14 Gans & 14 riders sent to III C.R.O. for road work at LE MENSIL. All sections vehicles in whip & driving drills. FANSHAWE-CUP to be played with No 5 Div. Team. D.A.C. lost 56 reinforcements arrived. Lt. FISHER to hospital.	
	4th "		C.O. & Adjt. to detailed portion of No 2 Sect'n at BOUCLY. B.Sch. moved to LE MENSIL to be near road work R. Near gathering line on Rt. Limes started. C.O. to TINCOURT. Adjt. to B.Sch. re road work. Lt. CONEY rejoined from leave 42 D.A.C. on A.R.P. at VILLERS FAUCON. 9 reinforcements sent to 46 A.S.P.	
	5th "		C.O. to B.Sch. at 6 A.M. to see road work commenced. C.O. round Sections. Adjt. to 45 R.A.H.Q.	
	6th "		C.O. round Sections & line to R.A.H.Q. Ch. parade 6.30 p.m. C.O. to B.Sch.	
	7th "		C.O. Adjt. & M.O. to B.Sch. for A.V.R. parade at 7 A.M. 30 O.R. reinforcements sent to 24	Bde - 5 officers (Mrs SELLERS, BATCHELOR, ROWDEN, FLETCHER, MERRYWEATHER) & 30 O.R. to 45 Army T.M. School at STE EMILIE portion No 2 Sect's at BOUCLY detached for line. No 1 Sect at STE EMILIE. O.C. 2nd Sect'n moved with half gun section to join his Half gun section at STE EMILIE. O.C. 2nd Sect'n moved portion No 2 Sect's at BOUCLY & detached for BUIRE to join his half gun section at BOUCLY. S.A.A. portion of Echelon remained at BUIRE	
	8th "		O.C. 1st Sect moved with half gun section to BUIRE from his half gun section at BOUCLY. Adjt. to STE EMILIE & BOUCLY. with half gun section to France Capt. ANDERSON commands 45 D.A.C.	
	9th "		C.O. (Capt. ANDERSON) to B.Sch. Mobilisation commenced by M.O. 4 and WARD. C.R.A. left 45 D.A.C.	
	10th "		Half No 1 gun section & half No 2 gun section returned to BUIRE from STE EMILIE & BOUCLY — respectively. C.O. & Adjt. round No 1 Section. Lt. CULVERWELL rejoined from hospital.	
	11th "		C.O. to B.Sch. Adjt. to R.A.H.Q. Remainder of No 1 Sect'n at STE EMILIE & remainder of No 2 Section at BOUCLY rejoined 1st & 2nd Sections respectively at BUIRE.	
	12th "		Adjt. at F.G.C.M. Adjt. to No 1 & 2 Sections.	
	13th "		Horse rugs, web clothing etc collected from Bdes for return to Ordnance Stores. C.O. & Adjt. to No 1 & 2 Sects & B.Sch. Capt. S.G. COOPER attached R.A.H.Q. Capt. BURBIDGE in command of No 2 Sect'n. B.Schultn stopped working on roads.	
	14th "		Horse rugs, web clothing to be returned to Ordnance Stores at PERONNE. B.Schultn moved from LE MENSIL to BUIRE.	
	15th "		C.O. & Adjt. round Sections. Horse rugs, web clothing re collected from Bdes & returned to Ordnance Stores at PERONNE. C.O. & Adjt. with No 2 Sect.	
LE TRANSLOY	16th "		Adjt. took billeting party to meet S.C.R.A. at BEAULENCOURT. 45 D.A.C. marched from BUIRE to LE TRANSLOY via TINCOURT — TEMPLEUX-LA-FOSSE — MOISLAINS (loading road line) — MANANCOURT — MENSIL — ROCQUIGNY.	
	17th "		C.O. to see O.C. 1st ANZAC D.A.C. & arranged to relieve them. Lt. CONEY & dump party sent to A.R.P. at BEUGNY. Adjt. to see 1st ANZAC D.A.C. & A.R.P. at BEUGNY with reference to relief by 45 D.A.C. Lt. LINES to FREMICOURT & alt ? Corps as Corps Hayhand Officer. Lt. SELLERS, BATCHELOR, ROWDEN, FLETCHER & MERRYWEATHER rejoined from 45 Army T.M. School also 30 O.R. Capt PEARCE on leave. Capt BURBIDGE to VELU as Officer in charge of waiting arrangements for Batteries.	

Army Form C. 2118.

WAR DIARY
or
INTELLIGENCE SUMMARY.
(Erase heading not required.)

Vol. XXX
M74. 1917.
(Contd.)

Instructions regarding War Diaries and Intelligence Summaries are contained in F.S. Regs., Part II. and the Staff Manual respectively. Title pages will be prepared in manuscript.

Place	Date	Hour	Summary of Events and Information	Remarks and references to Appendices
LE TRANSLOY	18th MAY		Genl. STRONG, C.R.A. 48 Div. inspected No 1 Sectn lines. Adjt to ARPs at BEUGNY.	
	19th "		48 D.A.C. relieved 1st ANZAC D.A.C. & took over A.RPS at BEUGNY. C.O. & Adjt to ARPs & round all Sections.	
HAPLINCOURT	20th "		48 D.A.C. moved from LE TRANSLOY to HAPLINCOURT. Route. BEAULENCOURT — VILLERS-AU-FLOS. C.O. & Adjt to ARP. Commenced moving ARP from I.22.a.7.0 & I.21.B.2.2 (Map 57c) C.O. inspected camp. A & rama & SCRA & see C.O. re removal of A Sectn to filter positn.	
	21st "		Adjt to see O.C. 10th Sect. 5th ANZAC DAC will refuse to relieving him. Adjt & party to prepare RApts C.O. & Adjt to ARPs & reconnoitred new positions for A Sectn & H.Q. 48 DAC. 10. G.S. wagons to RES at VELU wiring & repairs. 11 men received from hospital for Brigades. Capt MORRIS relieved Capt SMITH as M.O. 48 DAC.	
BEUGNY	22nd "		Adjt to see O.Hen Ya 5th ANZAC DAC Amm. dump at BEAULENCOURT & to arrange relief by us D.A.C. H.Q. 48 DAC moved to BEUGNY & A Sectn moved to I.27.c (57c) South of BEUGNY. C.O. returned from leave. Capt ANDERSON returned to B Sectn. Lt. CULVERWELL & party went to BEAULENCOURT to relieve 5 ANZAC DAC of Amm. dump. 6 G.S. & RE. s at VELU for wire.	
	23 "		Adjt to Ammunition dump at BEAULENCOURT, taken over from 5th ANZAC DAC C.O. & round Section. 6 G.S. to VELU on wire work.	
	24 "		C.O. & Adjt to R.A.H.Q. & to B Sectn. C.O. inspected No 1 & 2 Sections Lines & camp.	
	25 "		Lt. J. Mulligan. R.A.F.D.A.C. goes on leave and S.M. Ashbolt takes on his duties. A/Capt C.O. inspects lines & camp 57a A & B. Echol. 2M. Convoy types of grenade dump at BEUGNY. Projectiles of H.Q. A & B Ech. & C.R.A. & distinguished from M.D.effort to Capt M. Inglebery. Brigades BRE. & VELU for wire.	
	26 "		Adjutant outside lines. C.O. meets camp. C.M.E.S.G. & see men dentist or somelhing. No 93 Waggon to BEAUMETZ to move D.T.M.B. & recondl. O.C. inspects lines / No 1 Sect. Brigades to REATVELU forwire.	
	27th "		Adjt inspects filed lines, moved rest of Grenade dump at I.25 to my to prevent dump at BEUGNY At attack. & E.L. Lessons for RE. malloys hit to Bgde. 10 English learning / No 1 Sect. Brigades to English to work on RE. &c. at VELU in wire.	
	28th "		Capt Wilson inspects filled lines. Bragades with APP received and taking charge. Brigades to REATVELU. Caft Wilson returns to ARP. The Div Gunl minister moved into lines. The D.T.M.B. to Polo & scale C.R.A.	
	29th "		O.C. & No 6 Camp and lines. I/A & B Ech, to look at horses outside for a forale observation & arts to Polo. Natives? A.P.M. Div Messined No2 Gest set his knowing / two years hard some few & stencils & metholiate metholiate waved from Labour Land & loathead BAPAUME. Co + and greet, photball motor lounge	
	30 "		Convoy & Capt. Ind & lines N.A.D. at wash camp at NN.45.d at 6.30pm to be removed of allowance of different dump N 135. V. & N.Y.29. Bragade to RES at VELU to wire Capt of 135 V.G.N.Y.29. the inexplicable & locations BAPAUME. Bragade to RES at VELU to wire dump at 135 V.G.N.Y.29. the inexplicable A.E.L. 2H Wagons & SAA wagons from dump at M.11.d & O-Scum Ave REBANK 10 wagons	
	31st "		from R.E. at WFEL. to wire C/H. PEARCE returns from leave	

J.B. Hobart Major
D.V.L. AMMUNITION COLUMN.

CONFIDENTIAL.

WAR DIARY OF

48th (S.M.) DIVISIONAL

AMMUNITION COLUMN. R.F.A.

FROM 1st JUNE 1917 TO 30th JUNE 1917.

(VOLUME XXXI.)

WAR DIARY or INTELLIGENCE SUMMARY

Army Form C. 2118.

HEADQUARTERS, 48th (S.M.) DIVISIONAL AMMUNITION COLUMN.
Volume XXX/
Date 30/6/17

Place	Date 1917	Hour	Summary of Events and Information	Remarks and references to Appendices
BEUGNY	JUNE 1st		CO & 7/Adjt visit camp & lines of A.Sch. QOCRA. IV Corps visits HQ lines & camp & A.R.P. 10.A.S. wagons to R.E. WOR at VELU.	
	" 2nd		C.O. visits Sections 1 & 2. Horse shows in afternoon. D.A.C. win 2 classes out of 3. 10 A.S. wagons to R.E. work at VELU until daily until further notice.	
	" 3rd		C.O. visits Sections in morning. Ch. Parade at A.Sch lines 10 a.m.	
	" 4th		C.O. & 7/Adjt visit camps of A+B Schs. Adjt is ARP's Grenade & Salvage dumps. Dist: Barrel & Capt in A.Sch. lines during morning. C.O./Adjt is B Schat 10p.m. Kit LINES proceeded on leave.	
	" 5th		C.O. visits camps & lines of A+B Schs. 10 A.S. wagons employed all day on Salvag Amun "	
	" 6th		C.O. & 7/Adjt visit camps & lines of A+B Sch. BCBR moved to B.(Gray)	
	" 7th		C.O. visits Aschn camp & lines. 1/7 9.45 H.T.M & 10.R.O. and 9.45 " moved to D.T.M.O at BEAUMETZ.	
	" 8th		C.O. & 7/Adjt is A+B Schs. 2/Lt. BATCHELOR posted to 2nd Bde. Lt. MERRYWEATHER is duty with B Sch. from No 2. Sect. 4 horses collect defect. ammunition from Salvage dump BEAULENCOURT to return to railhead 3. A.S. to collect R.E. material for D.T.M.O.	
	" 9th		C.O. & 7/Adjt visit lines & camp of B.Sch. 14 men from 105th ANZAC D.A.C. to aid in ARP, 10 A.S. to be sent to FREMICOURT stone dump daily for road making & until further orders, also 3 GS. for 25B T. Capt R.E. at DELSAUX FME on Riley at 8 am on this order. 2 G.S. wagons for R.E. material for D.T.M.O. 2/Lt O.R. 2 enter & men (5 ORs) joined from base. Lt. BISHOP appointed IV Corps Agricultural Officer. 2/Adjt (2/Lt HOBSON) left to join IV Corps. Hy. Course. Cl. Parades B.Sch. 11.30 AM (Rch. Serm Gen'l Sir R. FANSHAWE KCB present. C.O. inspected all dumps. Rec'd notification to salve all farming implements. Telegram rec'd from Adjt stating he was at 27 I.B.D. awaiting a board crossing. C.O to Camp & 15 men sent to Seaside Rest Camp. A.D.Vs inspected all section lines.	
	" 10th		R.A.H.Q. Enquired who drank of a mule which was killed by a train a level crossing. C.O. to R.A.H.Q. C.O. asked for a shell red Ordnance Officer to arrive Vmpreat side of all dumps Adjt returned from leave. SCRA & see dumps to visit C.O. C.O. judged at 240 Bde horse shows	
	" 12th		C.O. & Adjt visited all sections. Adjt visited dumps. Capt MORRIS R.A.M.C. HO 4c Bde Ltd 3 weeks leave.	
	" 14th		C.O & Adjt to B Sch. Oail to SALVAGE dump at BEAULENCOURT to railhead at BAPAUME. Gross.	

A 5834 Wt. W4973/M687 750,000 8/16 D.D. & L. Ltd. Forms/C.2118/13.

Army Form C. 2118.

WAR DIARY
or
INTELLIGENCE SUMMARY.
(Erase heading not required.)

Instructions regarding War Diaries and Intelligence Summaries are contained in F. S. Regs., Part II. and the Staff Manual respectively. Title pages will be prepared in manuscript.

HEADQUARTERS,
48th (S. M.) DIVISIONAL AMMUNITION COLUMN.
VOLUME XXXI
No.
Date 30/6/17.

Place	Date	Hour	Summary of Events and Information	Remarks and references to Appendices
BEUGNY	June 14 (cont'd)		Country race from BEUGNY to HAPLINCOURT for Cup presented by Capt FARRELL A.V.C. won by Lt. BARRATT 1st Sect. 48 D.A.C. H'd to D.A.C. winning team. Lt. H.D. LINES returned from leave. Major SUMMER HAYES, D.S.O, R.A.M.C. took over duties as M.O.	
"	15		C.O. to N°2 Sect. Adjt to N°2 1+2 Sect. from Lts. TUCKER & FISHER sent on 5th Army Art Course. Lt. MERRYWEATHER posted to 49 Div Arty. IV Corps. Cmdr. visited N°1 Sect & expressed pleasure. Lt. LINES to command N°2 Sect.	
"	16		Adjt to BEAULENCOURT Salvage dump. C.O. & Adjt to 240 Bde Spares. Competition between Sects 1 & 2 for best Turnout o'draw. C.O. noted B.Sch. in evening. B. Schelen lost 2 mules from lines. C.O. Parade B.Sch. at HAPLINCOURT at 11.30 A.M. Ch. Parade at 6 p.m. Adjt inspected ammunition dump. D.A.C. warned to do all we can in way making horses fit for P.O. selected suitable Hay Land.	
"	17		Saddles received from Ordnance & haymaking commenced. C.O. to R.A.H.Q. Adjt to BEAULENCOURT Salvage dump. Capt COOPER & Lt AUNYON returned from leave. Capt COOPER remained at td R.A.H.Q. B.Sch. dumped old gun ammunition at A.R.P. 1780 fuzes 106 received	
"	18		Capt S.A. COOPER returned to duty with DAC from R.A.H.Q. Adjt to BIHUCOURT.	
"	19		200 rounds BX sent to 42 D.A.C. at RUYAULCOURT. Lt GRUNDY on leave. 3 G.S. wagons to D.T.M.O. to withdraw T.M. Batteries. C.O. & S.CRA reconnoitre Breelen near MAMETZ. Adjt to B.Sch. + to BEAULENCOURT Salvage dump.	
"	20		Busy refilling battery wagon lines. Lt LINES + 14 O.R. to AUXI-LE-CHATEAU to fetch h.G.S. & horses for Div. Sect. Cmdrs Conference at H'Q at 9 A.M. C.O. to R.A.H.Q. Adjt visited ARPS 56 D.A. had von guns to 1st ANZAC D.A. at 48 D.A.C. H'Q. Capt. COOPER member of F.G.C.M.	
"	21		Sect Cmndr & Adjt reconnoitre camps at BOTTOM WOOD near MAMETZ. Advance parties (take over camps) dis-infect billets & evict water troughs. Lt LINES returned with h.G.S. & horses from AUXI-LE-CHATEAU & delivered then to Div. Capt COOPER att'd R.A.H.Q.	
"	22		Sect Cmndr's Conference att'd at 9 A.M. A.R.P. Gas shell dump & Parade dump (also at BEUGNY) + Salvage dump at BEULENCOURT & all Carts built to be had at our disposal. Major DAC which relieved 48 D.A.C. at 12 noon. Capts. LYONS & J.B. BROWNE to tp. MAJOR (a is within hour) T.M. (T.F.C. from action) arrived from BEUGNY + HAPLINCOURT 48 D.A.C. (also 10 G.S. wagons to complete established of T.M. Battery.)	
"	23			
BOTTOM WOOD near MAMETZ	24		Area to BOTTOM WOOD near MAMETZ via FREMICOURT, BAPAUME, BABAUME - ALBERT Road, LA BOISSELLE CONTALMAISON FRICOURT, MAMETZ. left BEUGNY 5.20 A.M. arrived BOTTOM WOOD 12.50 p.m. G.O.C. Div. inspected Column in march through BAPAUME. CRA + staff visited camp. Lt CONEY arrived 8.30 pm with 1 D.G.S. wagons Ltd.	
"	25		Lt. CULVERWELL & party to ACHIET-LE-GRAND to collect 50 L.D.	
"	26		Lt CULVERWELL & party returned with remounts.	
"	27		Lt STEDMAN & WARHAM joined from base as reinforcements. S.CRA distributed remounts. Lt CONEY & party procured on leave. C.R.A inspected N°2 Sect. Lines	
"	28		2. 18 pdr. + 1. 4.5" How. rec'd from 341 Bde for training & Lt. STEDMAN posted to D/240 & Lt. WARHAM to C/241.	

WAR DIARY
INTELLIGENCE SUMMARY.

Army Form C. 2118.

HEADQUARTERS,
48th (S. M.) DIVISIONAL
AMMUNITION COLUMN.
VOLUME XXXI
No.
Date 30/6/17

Place	Date	Hour	Summary of Events and Information	Remarks and references to Appendices
BOTTOM WOOD near MAMETZ	June 29		Gundrill & rifle firing for NCOs & men.	
"	" 30"		Capt COOPER to RATHR & to see AREA COMMANDANT. Gundrills. Adjt inspected camp. Camp Commander to inspect a new camp.	

F. Moltram br Adjt.
46. D.A.C.

CONFIDENTIAL
Vol 28

WAR DIARY.
FOR
48th (S.M.) DIVISIONAL AMMUNITION COLUMN R.F.A.

FOR THE MONTH OF JULY. 1917.

VOLUME. XXXII

HEADQUARTERS,
48th (S. M.) DIVISIONAL
AMMUNITION COLUMN.
No. 1.
Date 8. 1917.

Army Form C. 2118.

HEADQUARTERS,
46th (S. M.) DIVISIONAL
AMMUNITION COLUMN.

No. Volume XXII
Date July 1917

WAR DIARY
or
INTELLIGENCE SUMMARY.
(Erase heading not required.)

Instructions regarding War Diaries and Intelligence Summaries are contained in F.S. Regs., Part II and the Staff Manual respectively. Title pages will be prepared in manuscript.

Place	Date	Hour	Summary of Events and Information	Remarks and references to Appendices
BOTTOM WOOD nr. MAMETZ.	1st July		Capt COOPER + Adjt to LE SARS. Gundrille training continued. Ch. Parade 3 p.m.	
"	2nd "		C.O. + Adjt to R.A.H.Q. Gundrille, musketry practice. C.O. inspected all men in Nos 1 + 2 Sections.	
"	3rd "		C.O. inspected all men of BSch. C.O. + Capt ANDERSON to R.A.H.Q. Capt. COOPER + Lt R.A.H.Q. as Orderly Officer.	
"	4th "		All Officers attend Q.O.C. Div's Conference at R.A.H.Q. Adjt to BEAUSSART. Capt. BURBIDGE granted 1 month's leave to ENGLAND.	
BEAUSSART.	5th "	5.0 A.M.	D.A.C. moved from BOTTOM WOOD to BEAUSSART via MAMETZ — FRICOURT — ALBERT — AVELUY — MARTINSART + ENGLEBELMER. Halt supply at BEAUSSART Road.	
THIEVRES.	6th "	7.0 A.M.	D.A.C. moved from BEAUSSART to THIEVRES via BERTRANCOURT — BUS + AUTHIE.	
CANETTEMONT	7th "	11.0 A.M.	D.A.C. moved from THIEVRES to CANETTEMONT via ORVILLE — AMPLIER — AUTHEULE — DOULLENS — HAUTE VISÉE — BOUQUEMAISON — ARBRE Crossroads + REBREUVETTE —	
ROELLECOURT.	8th "	5.15 A.M.	D.A.C. moved from CANETTEMONT to ROELLECOURT via HOUVIN — MONCHEAUX — BUNEVILLE — MAISNIL ST POL + FOUFFLIN-RICAMETZ.	
"	9th "		Rested 1 day, at few STRONG visited BSch lines.	
NEDON + NEDONCHELLE	10th "		D.A.C. moved from ROELLECOURT to NEDON (1st Sect) + NEDONCHELLE (H.Q. 2nd Sect + BSch) via ST POL, VALHUON, TANGRY — SAINS-LES-PERNES + FIEFS.	
BOESEGHEM	11th "		D.A.C. moved from NEDON + NEDONCHELLE to BOESEGHEM via AMETTES — AMES — LIÈRES — ST HILAIRE — LAMBRES + AIRE. Capt. G.B LUCAS joined D.A.C. from 240 B.A.R.F.A.	
STAPLE.	12th "	8.45	D.A.C. moved from BOESEGHEM to STAPLE via LA BELLE HOTESSE + WALLON CAPPEL. (Capt WARHAM + Lts PIKE + EARLE joined from base.)	
STEENVOORDE	13th "		D.A.C. moved from STAPLE to STEENVOORDE via LONGUE CROIX + ST SYLVESTRE CAPPEL.	
PESELHOEK.	14th "		D.A.C. moved from STEENVOORDE to wagon lines near PESELHOEK via BEAUVOORDE + ABEELE HILLEHOEK + POPERINGHE. Capt COOPER completed billeting for Divisional Artillery to line 5 July with D.A.C. Lt CONEY returned from leave.	
"	15th "		C.O. held Sect Commdrs. conference. Lts FISHER + JUCKES returned from 5th Army Art. School. Working Party 1 Officer + 40 men sent to report to XVIII Corps Camouflage Officer.	
"	16th "		C.O. + Adjt round all Sections. C.O. + Adjt to see MODEL of 4th Divl Art zone. Material collected + delivered to D.T.M.O.	
"	17th "		Adjt reconnoitred Gallery positions. C.O. to conference at R.A.H.Q. 29 Divn. Adjt to S. Capt. A.R.P. D.A.C. Conveyance to LA BASSÉE — Supply to La Kreule. Adjt to R.A.H.Q. 4 Divn.	

Army Form C. 2118.

WAR DIARY
or
INTELLIGENCE SUMMARY
(Erase heading not required.)

HEADQUARTERS,
48th (S. M.) DIVISIONAL
AMMUNITION COLUMN.

No. Volume XXXII
Date July 1917.

Instructions regarding War Diaries and Intelligence Summaries are contained in F. S. Regs., Part II. and the Staff Manual respectively. Title pages will be prepared in manuscript.

Place	Date	Hour	Summary of Events and Information	Remarks and references to Appendices
PESELHOEK	18 July		C.O. Sound Sections C.O. + Adjt to S. Corps Amm Park. 2 mules killed + 2 men wounded at B/240 Bty position. Camouflage drawn from Corps Camn. on/Cage Officer + delivered to Bty positions. 2 G.S. wagons placed at disposal of Pack Battery duty.	
	19		40 reinforcements arrived from base. Lt HOBSON rejoined from IV Corps Inf. School. C.O. Sound Sections. Pack Saddle Transport Company of 60 mules formed in D.A.C. for use in passing over rough ground two mule tr. wheel traffic. Small A.R.P. formed near wagon line to supply 48 Div Inf. Lt TUCKES in charge.	
	20		C.O. reconnoitred Bty positions. Reinforcements (40) arrived. M.O. examined new Medical Officer C.O. Sound Sections. M.O. Adjt inspected Rations + cookhouses. No 82604 W. CLARK. S.S. suffered self inflicted wound. Parade of Pack Transport Corps.	
	21		Working party 50 men + 2/Lt FISHER sent to assist B/240 Bty -	
	22		Lt CONEY commenced forming forward Amm Dump on YSER canal Bank at C26c23 (Sheet 28) 40 reinforcements sent to Bdes. C.O. inspected Pack T. Corps. 40 men working party to 240 Bde.	
	23		Capt ANDERSON posted to D/240 Bty. Capt PEARCE ditto A/241 Bty. Gas shell received + issued to Batteries Capt LUCAS commands 15" Sec'n during absence of Capt PEARCE. Lt LINES commands B. Ech -	
	24		Lt CONEY could forming forward dump. Major SUMMERHAYES, B.S.O. R.A.M.C.T, 2/Lt D/T.C. 16 1 or 2 S.M. Fld. Amb. Capt MORRIS, R.A.M.C.T. Returned from leave. 2/Lt CONEY can ta forming forward dump	
	25		Adjt to S. Corps Amm Park. Lt TUCKES posted to D/241. Lt PYKE takes over charge of A.R.P. Lt CONEY can. tues forming forward dump.	
	26		Padre ASH joined for attachment, Adjt + Sec'n Commdrs reconnoitred forward wagon lines.	
	27		C.O. + Adjt to conference at 39 D.A.	
	28		C.O. + Adjt reconnoitred forward wagon lines. (Then 6 + 8 D.A.H.O. DAC filled to complement of Amm.	
	29		Party under C.O. clean YSER canal of dead horses. 12 reinforcements drawn posted to B/240. Adjt to advanced wagon line. Lt GUNYON + 20 men clean up D/241 position. Lt CONEY establishes a new dump on the track from IA bridge to HILL TOP FARM. 6 horses sent to B/240. C.O. sees the "Track" dump.	
	30		Party with Lt CONEY + pack mules under Lt HOBSON on line to dump ammunition in "Track" dump. Adjt + Capt LUCAS to advanced wagon line	
	31	7·30 A.M.	D.A.C. moved from PESELHOEK to VLAMERTINGHE. A Schelon supply "Track" dump. B Sch. mobile establishment dumped at A'fch for emergency. Adjt to Track dumps to B Schelon + XVIII Corps R.P.	

E. Waltham Hoyt
Col.
48 Div Amm Col.

War Diary

August 1917

48th (SM) Divisional Ammunition Column RFA

Volume XXXIV

WAR DIARY
INTELLIGENCE SUMMARY

Army Form C. 2118.

Place	Date 1917 Aug.	Hour	Summary of Events and Information	Remarks and references to Appendices
VLAMERTINGHE	2nd	—	C.O. to TRACK dump. Lt. PYKE & party relieve Lt. CONEY & party. Lt. CULVERWELL posted to T.M.S. Capt. PEARCE evacuated gassed.	
	3rd	—	Adjt. to S.C.R.A. to TRACK dump & HILLTOP FME. Faenus collectie relieving to batteries for gun platforms. Attacks dumped complement of gun amm'n. 737 B.K. by B.Sch. & 1000 4.5" charges to TRACK dump. Pack mule transport supplied to batteries. Adjt. to B.Sch. C.R.I. to see C.O.	
	4th	—	Lt. EARLE transferred to 50 D.A. Adjt. to TRACK dump. Atch dump complement of gun amm'n. to TRACK dumps. C.O. round Nos 1 & 3 Sechs. 201 reinforcements arrived & distributed. 240 Bn 59. 20 B.n. 13. TM. 10. DKC 89.	
	5th	—	[?]SINGTON & Lt. SYMINGTON reported. (Posted Nos 1 & 3 Sechs). No Pack mule. C.O. to B.Sch. Pack mule transport supplied to Batteries. Capt. BURBIDGE returns from leave & adjt. B.Sch. Adjt. to TRACK dump. Atch dump 2400 4.5" gun amm'n. & TRACK dump. Pack mule transport supplied to Batteries. C.O. to Div HQ. Lt. SIMPSON, WILSON & JAMES reported from 50 D.A. C.O. to R.A. HQ. Lt. PYKE relieves Lt. CONEY at TRACK dump.	
	7th	—	C.O. round Nos 1 & 3 Sechs. Lt. STANSFIELD WILSON & JAMES posted to 241 Bde. Lt. FISHER to 2/10 Bde. Capt. LUCAS to command B.Sch. Capt. WARHAM to command No.1 Sect. W.C.A. BELL reported from R.E. for duty.	
	8th	—	C.O. & Adjt. to TRACK dump. Lt. SIMPSON to assist A.P.M. in TRAFFIC CONTROL. Atch dump Railway Coaling TRACK dump. 1045 daily ex R.E. WGR. 4 Rations and from 3rd S.M. Field amt., fr 1st Rdn from wi D. S.G. Cap.	
	9th	—	C.O. & Adjt. to B.Sch. Has to Dm Bomb th from S.T.A. Supply. Atch 1 journey to TRACK dump. 199 Rounds ammunition from PROVEN for Div. Atch do 1 journey to TRACK dump.	
	10th	—	Lt. BELL to Hospital. Adjt to B.Sch. Run outs for D.A. distributed by AMMANBANK & THWAITES via D.M.	
	11th	—		
	12th	—	C.O. & Adjt. to TRACK dump. Div Grenade Store. EKST 1 CANAL BANK (H.31.d.9.) Taken over by DKC. Ch parade Arch. 8.30 AM.	
	13th	—	B.Sch. 6.30pm. TRACK dump skilled. 30 to 150 amm B.Sch.	
	14th	—	Atch to field Cashier. C.O. to TRACK dump. Adjt. to B.Sch. & PESELHOEK RE dm p. Rear amm'n salved from 3rd H.S. D.A. pos. dine & labour furnished to TRACK dm p. Atch 1 journey to TRACK dump.	
	15th	—	0.5 m.m. to Dv B.O. DTM. O. & CRE. Adjt. to TRACK dump. 1500 A.S. to TRACK dump. Atch. 1 Gs.to TRACK dump. Reinforcement Officers arrived & dis etc. 14 wks. WORKSDAH, KP 1 Sect. Lt. WHATNALL & ROOK 2 Sect. Lt. CRITCHLOW & CHAPMAN R.C. Sect.	
	16th	—	C.O. to TRACK dump at 11.45 AM (Zero Again). 5 Tunnels kingdom d disposed HILLTOPFM E, Kw. out Bn. 200 rounds with 4 Officers from 23 D.A. assist. One Pack Transport Amm. Lt. HOBSON Officer in admin.ch. STONES amm. to St. JULIEN. 5 drivers wounded. 3 mules killed. 45 mules evacuated. Lt. BISHOP returns from leave. Lt. RUNYON attd. 2nd Bde.	
	17th	—	Adjt. to TRACK dump. Atch. 2 journeys to TRACK dump. 2000 D.B.O. & CRE. 2500 AS to TRACK dm p.	

WAR DIARY
or
INTELLIGENCE SUMMARY.

(Erase heading not required.)

Army Form C. 2118.

Place	Date 1917	Hour	Summary of Events and Information	Remarks and references to Appendices
VLAMERTINGHE	18 Aug		10 A/S to C.R.E. 2 S.A.A. delivered by B.Sch. to TRACK dump. A/Sch. do 2 trips to TRACK dump. A/St. to B.Sch. Pack Mule Transport to Batteries.	
	19 -		10 A/S for C.R.E. A/Sch. 2½ trips to TRACK dump. Capt. 15 TRACK dump. Board of Enquiry on 2 missing mules. C.O. to R.A. H.Q. A/St. to Sen. XVIII Corps Camouflage Officer.	
	20 -		10 A/S to C.R.E. A/Sch. do 2½ trips to TRACK dump. Bdr Thompshot Mule to Battrs. C.O. inspected N°2 Sect on its road. 10 A/S CRE + D.B.O. A/St. inspected FCRM & BILLINGTON A/St. to B Sch. 100 Am. dumps collected from PROVEN.	
	21 -		A/Sch. do 2 journeys to TRACK dump. Also 1800 A/S to TRACK dump.	
	22 -		10 A/S CRE + D.B.O. A/Sch. 2½ trips to TRACK dump. 10 A/S CRE + DBO 275 from N°1 Sect. 48 D/HQ. Fur'd Rendevlers. C.O. to B Sch. A/Sch. for ALOSTER now. Capt. PRIDEAUX B/a/40 for ALOSTER now.	
	23 -		Following officers arrived to D/Section 2/Lts CROSSLING + BULLOCK N°1, SUMMERSALL + DOMAN N°2, LYSETT MERCER NEWBOLD + JONES B Sch. A/St. to TRACK dump. CO to R.A. H.Q. A/St. BILLINGTON awarded parcels to proceed EAST of I.H.K. for FGCM for self inflicted wound. Capt COOPER to see qr. prospect to proceed EAST of St JULIEN. A/Sch do 2 trips to TRACK dump.	
	24 -		Pack mules transport to Batteries. Capt. WARHAM to reco gas prospects to positn EAST of St JULIEN. 2 OR Killed on TRACK dump shelled. CO inspected N°1 Sect new area.	
	25 -		C.O. inspected N°2 Sect m mules. C.O. to TRACK dump.	
	26 -		A/C. Service 6:30 A.M. Café 10 A.M. A/Sch. to Stooks. to TRACK dump. A/St. to TRACK dump. CO to B Sch. Smoke case, P bombs + grenades delivered to Dump Forward Camouflage Dump. Stokes 3 Co. delivered to St. JULIEN.	
	27 -		2/Lts WORSDALL, CROSSLING, BULLOCK, WHATMAN, REDDY, CRITCHLOW CHAPMAN posted to 2/Lts B.Sch. 2/Lt SUMMERSALL to DOMAN, LYSETT, MERCER NEWBOLD + JONES to 2/H Batts - 6 A/S. to D/HQ 2 Lts 18/3/4/11. 145 Rem Dump/S collected from PROVEN. A/St. 2½ trips to TRACK dump.	
	28 -		A/St. prosecuted at FGCM. 31 Rem dumps collected from PROVEN. Amm. Salvage. 3000 N°1 + 5000 N°22 delivered to forward Dump. Forward dump. A/Sch. 15 to to TRACK dump.	
	29 -		CR.A. inspected N°3 1 + 2 sections. Empty cartridge cases cleared from batty positions.	
	30 -		Continued clearing batting positns for them + cartridge cases. 2 captured enemy guns collected from St JULIEN.	
	31 -		Continued clearing batting positns + empty cartridge cases. C.O. + A/St. to B.Sch. A/St. do 1 journey to TRACK dump. 2 AS Shell 7:30,000 8/16 dump + delivered to TRACK dump for D/2110. F. Wolfram Capt Adjt 45 D.K.C.	

WAR DIARY

For Month of September
—1917—

48th
Divl: Amma: Column. R.F.A.

—Volume No XXXV—

Vol 30

WAR DIARY or INTELLIGENCE SUMMARY

Army Form C. 2118.

Place	Date	Hour	Summary of Events and Information	Remarks and references to Appendices
VLAMERTINGHE	1st SEPT. 1917	—	Adjt. to TRACK dump. 241 Bty. positions continued to be cleared. A Col. 1 journey to TRACK dump.	
	2nd	—	BSM + BCER drawn for D/240 and delivered to TRACK dump. CAPT LUCAS & hospital. Church parade B Coy. 8.45 a.m.	
	3rd	—	2LTS SEARSON + HOBSON on leave. No 2 Sect. 1 journey to TRACK dump. D.O.V.S. orders 1 mule to be destroyed.	
	4th	—	Suspected EPIZOOTIC LYMPHANGITIS	
	5th	—	C.O. + Adj. to B Coy. + to R.A.H.Q. Salvage work continues.	
	6th	—	S.C.R.A. to see C.O.	
	7th	—	Adj. to B Coy + TRACK dump. 5 L.G.S. under Officer late gas projectors to ST. JULIEN. Salvage continues.	
		11.30pm	A Col. make 1 journey to TRACK dump. LT. SINGTON takes train to load men from XVII Corps dump to ADMIRALS ROAD. Enemy aeroplanes drop bombs in HLQrs + No 1 Sect. Lines following casualties :- KILLED Chapl. Rev. J. ASH. WOUNDED LT. COL. G.B. BROWNE D.S.O., CAPT. MOTTRAM, CAPT. HOPKINS (D.T.M.O.) + 8 other ranks. SLIGHTLY WOUNDED remainder at duty CAPT. MORRIS (R.A.M.C.) CAPT. J. WARHAM + 3 other ranks. CAPT. WARHAM takes over command.	
	8th	—	Padre ASH buried at VLAMERTINGHE. LT A.J. SINGTON to be acting Adjt. 2nd LT GRUNDY from dump to No 1 Sect. A Col. 2 journeys to TRACK dump. Salvage work continues. CAPT. MOTTRAM dies of wounds.	
	9th	—	Church Parade 10 a.m. Non C's taken by Padre MEAKE. Funeral of CAPT MOTTRAM at LOVIE CHATEAU.	
	10th	—	A Col. 1 journey to TRACK dump. LT-COL. H.L. TENNANT R.A. takes command of A.S.D.A.G. H.Qrs. Mos 1+2 Sections dig themselves in for protection against bombs from enemy air-craft which came over nightly.	
	11th	—	C.O. to No 2 Sect. Adj. to T.M. Camp. 46 gunners posted to Batteries. TRACK dump shelled. R.S.M. BROOM returns from leave.	
	12th	—	C.R.A. + No 1 Sect. visits T.M. Camp. Adjt. to B Coy. 1 6" Mortar taken to ST. JULIEN. 1 mule (No 2 Sect.) killed.	
	13th	—	250 rds. BX (Fuze 106) from XVIII Corps dump to D/241. 9 L.G.S. wagons carry for Z Special Coy. 4 R.E. to ST. JULIEN. C.O. to B. Coy. 26 Officers from Base LIEUT L.W.H. ROBINSON, 2LIEUT A.F. FLINT & posted No 1 Sect.	
	14th	—	500 rds BX (Fuze 106) from Corps dump to D/241. 2nd LIEUT GRUNDY + 4 N.C.O's to Vety Hospital (No 3) BOULOGNE. 2LTS SEARSON and HOBSON return from leave. Salvage work continued. 6 G.S. to C/240 to remove empties.	

Army Form C. 2118.

WAR DIARY
or
INTELLIGENCE SUMMARY.
(Erase heading not required.)

Instructions regarding War Diaries and Intelligence Summaries are contained in F. S. Regs., Part II. and the Staff Manual respectively. Title pages will be prepared in manuscript.

Place	Date	Hour	Summary of Events and Information	Remarks and references to Appendices
VLAMERTINGHE	15th SEPT		250 rds Bx (fuze 106) to D/241. 2Lt SEARSON appointed Salvage Offr. 2/Lts A.G. STEWART + H.A. CRYER report from 34th A.F.A. Bde + att. No 1 Sect. (dated previous 16th inst.). Barrage No 1 Sect shelled — no casualties.	
	16th		C.O/E service 240 Bde W.L. A col. 3 journeys to TRACK dump. B col. take 6 G.S. wagons with Fx. to C/240. 5 L.G.S. to ST JULIEN with gas projectors. 1 horse (No 1 Sect.) wounded. 1 dr (No 1 Sect.) accidentally wounded.	
	17th		4 Offrs from 146. B.A. vij :- LT. E.F. GRAHAM, 2/LT. F.A. PEPPER (Rein. to No 1 Sect.), 2/Lt L.S.S. DYER, LT. H.K. FOERS (Rein. posted No 2 Sect.). 30 pack mules to A/241. 12 H.W. wagons sent to D/240 new pos & hrs unable to reach pos. Bombs dropped on No 1 Sect lines. 2 men wounded, 5 horses wounded. All of No 1 Sect. Reinforcements arriving as following:-	
	18th	5.40 am	CAPT SMITH-CARRINGTON + 37 ORs ranks, posted to B col. 1 Gnr. 3—6 gunners to No 2 Sect. 1 mule (Btn) destroyed. 6 18pr wagn. loads from B/240 W.L. to Big pos. 432 rds Bx to D/241 from XVIII Corps dump. 12 wagn loads from K.O.C. dump to C/240. 320 rds A.S. from REIGERSBURG to A/241. 1dr (No 1 Sect.) 1dr (No 2 Sect) wounded. Adj. to TRACK dump. Horse ambulance given to 240 Bg pos" to clear emptoes. 16 reinforcements posted to 240 Bde.	
	19th		26 to 241 Bde. Reinforcement 2/LT. MYTTON – 2/LT. BRADSHAW from Base posted No 2 Sect. Posted to Brigade LT. GRAHAM, 2/LT FOERS – PEPPER to 240 Bde. 2/LTs DYER, STEWART, CRYER to 241 Bde.	
	20th		A col. journey to TRACK dump. LT. BISHOP to TRACK dump to relieve LT. AYRE. Difficulties of maintaining 1500 rds per gun REIGERSBURG empty. 6 wagns B/B/240, 6 wagns to C/240 with Ammn from K.O.C. dump. 30 pack mules	
	21st		C.O. to B col. 18 reinforcements posted 241 Bde, 15 to 240 Bde. 11 wagons with 8x to D/241.	
	22nd		Salvage continues daily. Adj. to A col. 6 18 pr wag no with ammn from K.O.C. dump. 7 wagons to A/241. 30 pack mules to B/245 new pos". 137 Gr Coal to taken from T.M. camp to K.O.C. dump.	
	23rd		Adj. to TRACK dump, + with 2 LT. SEARSON inspects progress of salvage work in roads + 240 Big pos. 505 rds D to C/240 new pos". (driver (No 2 Pdr) 18" for ammn. from ROGERS BURG to B/240 new pos". 505 rds B/240 new pos". wounded – 1 mule (No 2 Sect.) wounded missing Church Parade (with Commander) 240 (Bn. Div.	
	24th		1000 rds 18 pr from ROGERS BURG to A/240. 506 rds to A/241. 600 rds to B/241. 600 rds Sachieur, Lt. LINDT. OR to res pos. 1 6" T.M. field from ST. JULIEN. Scout Salvage done by all Sections returns from leave.	

Army Form C. 2118.

WAR DIARY
or
INTELLIGENCE SUMMARY.
(Erase heading not required.)

Instructions regarding War Diaries and Intelligence Summaries are contained in F.S. Regs., Part II. and the Staff Manual respectively. Title pages will be prepared in manuscript.

Place	Date	Hour	Summary of Events and Information	Remarks and references to Appendices
VLAMERTINGHE	25th SEPT.		600 rds. of B/241 from K.O.C. dump. 600 rds. from B/240 old to new posn. 80 L.D.H. + 11 L.D.M. arrested from PROVEN. Distributed at B Ech. L.D.H. to Brigades, 11 L.D.M. to Sections :- No 1 Sect 4, No 2 Sect 4, Brd. 3 1dr. (R Ech) killed, 1dr. (B Ech) wounded while on working party at B/126 posn. 2 N.C.O.'s + 40 men attached to 126 Bde since 11th inst. return. 2 Lt. GRUNDY + 4 N.C.O.'s return from No 3 1/26 Hosp. BOULOGNE.	
		8 PM	Bombs again dropped near Camp - no casualties	
	26th		Gwayno REGERSBURG dump to B/241. 4 wagons with 78 pr ammo from A/240 W.L. G Bty posn. Ammn Carriers Pack Saddles returned to Ordnance. 48 D.A.C. cease ammn supply from midnight 26th - 27th and is taken over by 18 B.A.C.	
	27th	11 AM	TRACK dump handed over to 18 D.A.C. East Sect's dump all gun ammn. S.A.A. ammn (except Grenades) in the lines and handed over to 18 B.A.C. Serve prolonged bombing attacks during night of 26th-27th. 1 man (No 2 Sect) Shell-Shock, 2 mules (No 2 Sect.) wounded. 2/Lt GRUNDY with S.C.R.A. to NORDPEENE as Billeting Offr. for 48.D.A.C.	
	28th	6 AM	D.A.C. move out with echelons to NORDPEENE rest area. Adj. with Advance Party from rch. Section + M. LANCKS met 2/Lt GRUNDY at NORDPEENE and arrange billets for all sections. Adj. visits toutes les C.O.'s + No 1 Sect.	
NORDPEENE	29th		C.O. and Adjt. visit all Sections. Mules very fit after 24 mile trek.	
	30th	9.30 AM	Voluntary C.O/E. Service at OCHTEZEELE. Adjt. to Nos 2+3 Sections.	

A.J.Sing? Lt.
Adj. 48 D.A.C.

A5834 Wt.W4973/M687 750,000 8/16 D.D.& L.Ltd. Forms/C.2118/13.

CONFIDENTIAL. Vol 3

War Diary

of

48" (SM) DIVISIONAL
AMMUNITION COLUMN. R.F.A

FOR

OCTOBER 1917

Volume XXXV

Army Form C. 2118.

WAR DIARY
or
INTELLIGENCE SUMMARY.
(Erase heading not required.)

Instructions regarding War Diaries and Intelligence Summaries are contained in F. S. Regs., Part II. and the Staff Manual respectively. Title pages will be prepared in manuscript.

HEADQUARTERS,
46th (S.M.) DIVISIONAL
AMMUNITION COLUMN.
No ....
Date 31/10

Place	Date	Hour	Summary of Events and Information	Remarks and references to Appendices
NOORDPENE	Oct 1st		32 Reinforcements arrive from Base. Capt Cooper G.R.A.H.Q. to act as S.C.R.A.	
	2nd		Reinforcements posted:- 12 to 240 Bde, 5 to 241 Bde.	
	3rd		Lt-Col. TENNANT proceeds on leave. Capt. WARHAM in Command.	
MINNEZEELE	4th		2/Lt GRUNDY proceeds on leave.	
	5th		48th D.A.C. move to WINNEZEELE area. T.M's attached for duty, discipline & rations. 26 Reinforcements arrive from Base.	
BRANDHOEK	6th		48th D.A.C. move to BRANDHOEK camp at G10d. (Sheet 28) (taken over from 9th B.A.C. Personnel & AMB dumps). VANCOUVER & MOAT FARM dumps relieved by 2 Officers 64 O.R's.	
	7th	3.30am	Severe bombing by enemy air-craft. Casualties:- Personnel Nil. Animals - killed & evacuated 36 (also 2 M.D. A.S.C. attached). Nos 1 & 2 Sections fill all amm.n wagons of 240, 241 Bde. Two Charges B.M. missing.	
	8th		Packing done for A/240, B/240, B/240 Batteries - 30 pack-mules, 1 N.C.O & 4 men sent to ORIHA dumps as guard.	
VLAMERTINGHE	9th		48th B.A.C. move to camp near VLAMERTINGHE (H.15.d. Sheet 28) vacated by Brigades. 14 wagons lead to rail. Bde to move the forward.	
	10th		Reinforcements posted to Brigades :- To 240 Bde 1 driver, 21 gunners. 5 Telephonists; To 241 Bde 4 drivers 7 gunners, 6 Telephonists. Much pack'y done. A,B,D Batteries (240 Bde) supplied.	
	11th		2/Lt CONEY proceeds on leave. 60 18pr and 252 4.5in carried down railed & Brigades. 40 mules do packed for A/240, 30 mules for B/240. 72 Remounts collected from WIPPENHOEK Railhead.	
	12th		10 Remounts (L.D.) issued to 241 Bde. 36 pack-mules for B/240, 50 pack mules to 241 Bde. 2 mules belonging to the Bac lost. Cont' d & giving relief x (a) 2 riding missing from Bdes (b) 2 H.Qs mules issuing in tech Case to due to injuries (twice). Personnel at dumps relieved by 46th DAC.	
	13th		Lt LINES % of Remount party of 74 O.R's proceeds to BOULOGNE to collect remounts for 46th DAC.	
EECKE	14th		48th BAC march & EECKE area. Inspected by C.R.A. on POPERINGHE-SWITCH Rd. 4.S. Swayne detailed to each Bde. Capt. LUCAS LUCAS returns from Leave.	
MORBECQUE	15th		March continued to MORBECQUE area. 1 vide horse (no 1 sect) left shire.	
VENDIN-LEZ-BETHUNE	16th		March continued to VENDIN-LEZ-BETHUNE. Lt-Col TENNANT and 2/Lt GRUNDY return from leave. Capt SMITH-CARRINGTON left at MORBECQUE with forage rations for remount party. Party return.	

T.M. Count

WAR DIARY or INTELLIGENCE SUMMARY

Army Form C. 2118.

HEADQUARTERS
46th (S. M.) DIVISIONAL
AMMUNITION COLUMN.
No. ....
Date 31/12

Place	Date	Hour	Summary of Events and Information	Remarks and references to Appendices
VENDIN-LES-BETHUNE	17th		48th D.A.C. move to ABLAIN ST NAZAIRE. 2/Lt BISHOP Offr a/VENDIN with four horses for Remount Party.	
ABLAIN-ST-NAZAIRE	18th		Adjt. to Camp of 2nd C.B.A.C. Camp at A.2 Central (Sheet 51b.) C.O. to Nos 1+2 Sections + Boesleux. Adjt. to R.A. HQ. at Camp FORT GEORGE and 2nd Can. D.A.C. 2/Lt. GRUNDY to be orderly Offr. Capt. WARHAM proceeds on leave.	
	19th	10am	LA TARGETTE dump, WINCHESTER DUMP - KING'S DUMP taken over from 2nd Can. B.A.C. 2/Lt SEARSON as Dump Officer at LA TARGETTE dump. 5 N.C.O's +16 men sent as guards to forward positions ammn is taken over. Remount Party arrives. Remounts distributed. S.A.C. 3 riders +68 mules + LT WILLIAMS' up to Bases +200 B troPln. C.O. to 2nd Can. B.A.C. Camp all ammn supply by Light Railway. Lt. VAUX reports from Base, attached No 2 Sect. Cpl. BURROUGHS up to from SMELLEN, att. No1 Sect. Adjt. to the S.C.R.A. WINCHESTER - KING'S dumps to be cleaned. Ammn ammn to the bright trench to LA TARGETTE dump from forward positions three files. Jump wgs drawn from Ordnance up to Establishment.	
	20th			
	21st		2/Lt GRUNDY to LA TARGETTE dump. Cleaning of WINCHESTER dump & Cabo. 1 N.C.O. +4 men as guard sent to BOX dump at MONT ST. ELOI.	
	22nd		Adjt. to MONT ST ELOI to inspect sites for white Camps for HQrs +Nos 1+2 Sections. 1 Sgt +20 men sent to LA TARGETTE dump as working party.	
LA TARGETTE	23rd		48 BAC. move to A 2 Central. Taking over from 2nd Can. D.A.C., 14 G.S. wagons +6-241 Bde for move.	
	24th		2/Lt HOBSON +20 OR's att. R. Group, 2/Lt MYTTON +20 OR's att. L Group to clear ammn at forward positions. 1 N.C.o + 9 men att. Ava Commandant NEUVILLE ST VAAST as billet wardens. 800 BX ammn to D/241, 200 BX to D/240. 2/Lt CANEY returns from leave.	
	25th		G.S wagon evacd. to B trophn. for hauling material for White Qui - 10 to 241 Bde, 2 to D/240. 20 pack mules for D/241. B.A.C. reorganized to new Wait Establishment. 2/Lt MOAY posted to Y/48 T.M.B	
	26th		Capt. SMITH-CARRINGTON +120 men to KING'S dump to clear same. H.Qs. + No 2 Sect. move to MONT ST ELOI at FQHt. (51 B.J.) 2/Lt. HOBSON +/Lt FLINT posted to Y/240 Bde; LIEUT VAUX and LIEUT ROBINSON to 241 Bde. LT LINES to command No 1 Sect. in Capt WARHAM's absence. S.A.A. Sect. drew SMA ammn up to Establishment. 20 pack mules for D/241.	

Army Form C. 2118.

WAR DIARY
or
INTELLIGENCE SUMMARY
(Erase heading not required.)

Place	Date	Hour	Summary of Events and Information	Remarks and references to Appendices
HQ MONT ST ELOI	Oct. 27th		S.C.R.A. & HQrs 48 D.A.C. Matured for men's accommodation drawn. Huts not finished busy constructing huts, building roads. 2/Lt GRUNDY to hospital. 2 wagons loaned to 3/240. Church Parade at No 2 Rest Camp at 4 P.M. Lt LIGHTBODY 477 Field (H) as Adviso F.Div Artillery for Musketry would guarante.	
	28th		1 B.G.S. wagons 1 Maltese Cart (Surplus to new establishment) and 37 mules in charge of Lieut. BISHOP went to ABBEVILLE, LIEUT MUMMERY and 2/Lt GOSS from Base to 1st Army Artillery School report no point to No 1 Sect.	
	29th		138 mules surplus to establishment issued to Rupembe, 69 to French Bde. Adj. & R.S.M. to all Sections to inspect woollen new Camps. 16 O.R's proceed to BOULOGNE with Div. Remount Pty. 14 signallers return from course at ZEGGERS CAPPEL	
	30th		4A TARGETTE & KING'S dumps sent 7200 lbs (AMMX) back to "A" Army Dump at CAMBLAIN 2/Lt GRUNDY returns from hospital. CAPT WARHAM returns from leave	
	31st		5 G.S. wagons to 2nd Bde. Mine surplus ammn. returned to "A" Army dump. Pedie/Ruskell/Lewis/Sports + attached to HQrs 48 D.A.C.	

O.V.Sey ln
ADJT.
48th DIVL AMMUNITION COLUMN.

www.ingramcontent.com/pod-product-compliance
Lightning Source LLC
Chambersburg PA
CBHW081237170426
43191CB00034B/1924